nextlist
2021

J.P.Morgan

IMPACT

Other books by the author

The Second Bounce of the Ball
ON IMPACT: A Guide to the Impact Revolution

IMPACT

Reshaping Capitalism to Drive Real Change

Sir Ronald Cohen

EBURY
PRESS

3 5 7 9 10 8 6 4

Published in 2020 by Ebury Press an imprint of Ebury Publishing,
20 Vauxhall Bridge Road,
London SW1V 2SA

Ebury Press is part of the Penguin Random House group of companies
whose addresses can be found at global.penguinrandomhouse.com

Text © Sir Ronald Cohen 2020

First published by Ebury Press in 2020

www.penguin.co.uk

A CIP catalogue record for this book is available from the British Library

ISBN 9781529108057

Typeset in 11.5/16.1 pt Slate Std
by Integra Software Services Pvt. Ltd, Pondicherry

Printed and bound in Great Britain by Clays Ltd, Elcograf S.p.A.

Penguin Random House is committed to a
sustainable future for our business, our readers
and our planet. This book is made from Forest
Stewardship Council® certified paper.

This book is dedicated to my dearest partners in this revolution, my wife, Sharon, our daughter and son-in-law, Tamara and Or, and our son, Jonny.

My warmest thanks go to my pioneering colleagues on the Social Investment Taskforce (2000–2010), at Bridges Fund Management (2002-), on the Commission for Unclaimed Assets (2005–07), at Social Finance worldwide (2007-), at Big Society Capital (2012–19), on the G8 Taskforce for Social Impact Investment (2013–14), at the Global Steering Group for Impact Investment (2015-), at the Impact Management Project (2016-) and at the Impact-Weighted Accounts Initiative (2019-). You are valiant comrades-in-arms, and it is thanks to your leadership, effort and vision that the Impact Revolution is here.

I also want to thank most warmly, my close colleague in researching this book, Yaelle Ester Ben-David, for her unflinching determination and steadfast support.

Dear Reader,

As this book goes to print, our economies are in lockdown because of the Corona virus. Huge sectors of our economies have come to a sudden stop, unemployment is rising to levels unseen since the Great Depression and stock markets have crashed. The strains on our economic and financial systems are likely to be orders of magnitude greater than those we experienced during the crash of 2008.

Across the world, the people worst hit, once again, will be the most vulnerable in our societies.

I hope the new thinking revealed in these pages will lead our governments to direct their massive economic measures in such a way that it creates the maximum positive social impact. Social justice must dictate our economic response to this grave crisis, so that we do not emerge from it with even greater pain, inequality and violent rebellion against the inequity of our system.

Ronnie

CONTENTS

INTRODUCTION

N early 20 years ago, I gave a speech at an event to celebrate the thirtieth anniversary of Apax Partners, the
venture capital and private equity firm I co-founded and led
for so many years. I warned then that if we did not tackle the
needs of those left behind more effectively, a 'curtain of fire'
would soon separate the rich from the poor in our cities, countries and continents. We have recently seen this curtain rise
in countries such as France, Lebanon and Chile, which have
suffered violent protests, while in the UK rising inequality was
a factor in the decision taken in the referendum of June 2016
to leave the EU.

Today, the gap between rich and poor has widened mas-
sively. Inequality is causing huge migration from poorer
countries, especially in Africa, to richer countries in Europe,
with people risking their lives to cross the sea in flimsy rubber
boats in search of better lives. The challenges arising from
absorbing these immigrants are exacerbating the inequalities
that already exist in the host countries.

I am writing this book because I can see that a solution is
within our grasp; I call it the 'Impact Revolution'. Fueled by
impact investment, it will allow us to address the dangerous
inequality and degradation of our planet, and will lead us to a
new and better world.

The journey that led me to write this book began in 1998, when I took the decision that seven years later, at the age of 60, I would leave Apax in order to tackle social issues and try to help resolve the conflict in the Middle East. I did not want my epitaph to read, 'He delivered a 30 per cent annual return on investment' – I'd always known that life should have a greater purpose.

When I was 11, my family and I were forced to leave Egypt and were lucky enough to be accepted by the UK as refugees. We arrived with just one suitcase each, me clutching my stamp collection under my arm, fearing that it would be taken away from me. We were made welcome in our new home and started to rebuild our lives in London.

I received several breaks in life, including a first-class education at Oxford and then at Harvard, where I discovered venture capital just as it was emerging. I received a Henry Fellowship, which paid for my first year at Harvard Business School but required me to bring something of value back to the UK after my studies. I ended up bringing back venture capital, for which I was knighted in 2001.

Giving back is an important aspect of my values. Just as I was helped when I was in need, I want to help others. Part of the reason I became a venture capitalist was that I knew it would enable me to help to create jobs at a time of high unemployment. As I saw social problems spreading during the 1980s and 1990s, I remained motivated to make a difference. I hoped that by leaving Apax at the age of 60, I could devote 20 years to these issues and have a chance to make a real difference.

I co-founded Apax when I was 26 and built it into a global private equity firm with offices across the world, and it now manages more than $50 billion.

Throughout my career, I have played many different roles: as an entrepreneur, as an investor, as a philanthropist and as an advisor to governments. Each of these roles has given me the opportunity to view the world from a different perspective. These experiences have led me to understand why capitalism is no longer answering the needs of our planet, and that there is a new way forward. In this book, I propose a new solution that we can each put into action.

Things cannot continue as they are. As inequality surges in developed and developing countries alike, social tensions rise and those who have been left behind feel that they will be permanently stuck there. Our system does not seem fair to them, and so they rebel against it.

At the same time, environmental challenges threaten the quality of life on the planet and possibly its very existence. Our current economic system cannot correct this threat: governments do not have the means to cope with our human-made social and environmental problems, nor are they well placed to develop innovative approaches to tackling them, a process that inevitably involves risky investment, experimentation and occasional failure.

The governments of countries in the Organization for Economic Co-operation and Development (OECD) are already spending more than $10 trillion every year on health and education; this is the equivalent to 20 per cent of their GNP, double what was spent 60 years ago. Governments are constrained by budgets and feel unable to spend more, and yet this is still not enough. Philanthropy can only do so much to help governments meet these challenges: philanthropic foundation donations stand at $150 billion each year globally, a small figure relative to government expenditure.[1]

There is, therefore, an obvious need for a new system, a need that has been publicly recognized by leading figures in finance and business. Until now, however, we have spent a great deal of time diagnosing our system's problems and precious little time proposing real alternatives to capitalism, leaving us feeling stuck, with no way forward.

Humankind *has* made enormous progress. We are capable of finding the right answer, of shifting to a new system that distributes opportunity and outcomes more fairly and proposes effective solutions to our great challenges. We need a new system where, for both moral and prudential reasons, a sense of mission reins in self-interest; where contribution confers greater status than conspicuous consumption; where firms that demonstrate social and environmental integrity are more successful than those that are simply self-interested; and where individuals and organizations are encouraged to find fulfilment in being part of something bigger than themselves, rather than in striving just to make money.

This new system is impact capitalism. It aligns the private sector with government, so that the two work in harmony rather than opposition, harnessing capital and innovation to solve social and environmental issues.

It attracts capital from investment markets, in much the same way as private capital has funded entrepreneurs to help bring about a revolution in technology over the last four decades.

It marries social and environmental impact with profit, overthrowing the tyranny of profit and placing impact firmly by its side, to keep it in check. It is already evident in our changed preferences: we are increasingly choosing to buy products from companies that share our values; we are investing in companies that do not pollute the environment or use child labor; and we are working in greater numbers for companies that have inspiring social or environmental goals.

The fuel of the capitalist system is capital, so it is not surprising that impact investing is a manifestation of the new system. Just as venture capital was the response to the investment needs of tech entrepreneurs, so impact investment is the response to the needs of impact entrepreneurs and businesses that want to improve lives and help the planet.

The Impact Revolution is already transforming the way we think about social responsibility, business models and investment. It is beginning to change our economies, turning them into powerful engines that drive capital to achieve impact alongside profit. We can already see it marking the twenty-first century as much as the Tech Revolution marked the twentieth.

Impact investing is about creating a chain reaction. One that brings innovation to the five groups of stakeholders we will examine in different chapters of this book, whose engagement is crucial to tackling massive social and environmental challenges at scale. One that changes the mindset and behavior of investors, philanthropists, entrepreneurs, social organizations, big business, governments and the general public and places impact at the center of our decision-making.

Much of the impetus for me to develop impact investment has stemmed from the work of the Social Investment Task Force (SITF), which I established in the UK in 2000 at the request of the UK Treasury.

Later in 2013, in light of the progress which had been made, the British prime minister David Cameron asked me to lead the G8 Social Impact Investment Taskforce (G8T), in order 'to catalyze a global market in social impact investment'. When Russia left the G8 in 2014, the geographic scope of the taskforce included the US, the UK, Japan, France, Italy, Germany and Canada, to which we added Australia and the European Union as observers. We set about organizing more than 200 people across these countries in eight national advisory boards and four working groups.

A striking conclusion emerged from our work: we realized that a deep change was occurring, as the world was shifting from one where decisions were made on the basis of risk and return to one where impact was an essential third dimension. The Social Impact Bond (SIB) – a new way of investing that 'did well' at the same time as 'doing good' – was the first expression of this fundamental change.

Our findings were articulated in a report, 'Impact Investment: The Invisible Heart of Markets', published in September 2014. It included the endorsement of figures ranging from Pope Francis, who urged governments 'to commit themselves to developing a market of high-impact investments and thus to combating an economy which excludes and discards', to the former US Treasury Secretary Larry Summers, who called it 'ground zero of a big deal'.[2] The report kicked off a movement to spread the idea across the world.

Soon after the report appeared, the British government asked me to lead the effort to expand the work of the G8T globally. And so in August 2015 I co-founded The Global Steering Group for Impact Investment (GSG) and took over as Chair to continue the work that the G8T had started. The GSG recruited most of the G8T Board members and quickly admitted five new countries: Brazil, Mexico, India, Israel and Portugal.

Under the leadership of Amit Bhatia, its inaugural CEO, the GSG expanded to 32 countries, engaging over 500 impact leaders across its national advisory boards. Driving to 'innovate, agitate and orchestrate'[3] at the same time, it has become the leading force advancing the progress of impact investment across the world.

In 2007, I felt that something fundamental was changing in the world. I could tell that social investment would be the next big thing and wrote about it in my first book, *The Second Bounce of the Ball*. Now, more than a decade later, I believe that impact thinking will bring about as great a change as that brought by the Tech Revolution.

Impact thinking is changing our investment behavior, just as innovative thinking about measuring risk did 50 years ago. Risk thinking resulted in portfolios whose risk is diversified across many different asset classes, allowing them to capture the high returns of higher-risk investments like venture capital and investment in emerging markets. Impact thinking will now transform our economies and reshape our world.

For me, the breakthrough in impact thinking came in September 2010, when for the first time we linked the measurement of social impact to financial return. The first social impact bond (SIB), the 'Peterborough SIB', tackled the reoffending rate of young male prisoners released from Peterborough jail in the UK. Until the arrival of SIBs, conventional wisdom had it that nothing in the social arena could be measured. How can you measure an improvement in the life of a prisoner who avoids going back to prison? With 192 SIBs and DIBs (Development Impact Bonds - SIBs that address challenges in developing countries) today tackling more than a dozen social problems in 32 countries, it has become clear that by linking improvements in social and environmental outcome to a financial return we can hand the keys to the investment market to leaders of charitable organizations. By doing so, we have given social entrepreneurs the financial freedom they lacked to develop innovative solutions to our biggest social challenges.

The creation of the SIB was an early sign of the impact innovation that is occurring today. Just like the software and hardware firms of the 1980s and 1990s, innovative 'impact' organizations, both non-profit 'social organizations' and 'purpose-driven businesses', are bringing creative disruption to the existing models of entrepreneurship, investment, big business, philanthropy and even government.

This book introduces a new theory about how the Impact Revolution will enable us to achieve systemic social and environmental improvement, and puts its progress in perspective. It examines the trends affecting different groups in our society and how these groups influence one another, creating momentum for change across our whole system.

Chapter 1 introduces the Impact Revolution and the innovative thinking that powerfully drives it: the triple helix of risk–return impact. It shows how the Impact Revolution resembles the Tech Revolution that preceded it.

Chapter 2 examines impact entrepreneurship and looks at how young entrepreneurs are redefining disruptive business models that improve lives and the planet, in addition to generating financial gain.

Chapter 3 addresses the role of investors, who are already driving businesses to integrate impact into their products and operations.

Chapter 4 turns to the effect of the Impact Revolution within big corporations. Influenced by the changing preferences of consumers, employees and investors, and sometimes by the business models of smaller competitors (discussed in Chapter 2), big companies are beginning to embed impact in some of their activities and product lines.

Chapter 5 considers the new model of philanthropy that is emerging in response to impact thinking and innovative impact tools. We look into the use of outcome-based philanthropy and foundation endowments to maximize improvement in lives and the environment.

Chapter 6 explores how impact approaches and tools can help governments solve bigger problems, faster.

Finally, Chapter 7 charts the way ahead. We cannot persist with a system that does not actively seek to make a positive impact, while at the same time it creates negative consequences that governments have to spend a fortune trying to redress. We must transform our economies so that they generate solutions rather than problems. And much is at stake – billions of people's lives depend on the success of the Impact Revolution. There has never been a more tangible opportunity to make a transformative difference, and each of us has a significant role to play in making it happen.

The economist Adam Smith famously introduced the 'invisible hand of markets' in *The Wealth of Nations* at the end of the eighteenth century, to describe how everyone's striving for profit results in everyone's best interests. His first book, *The Theory of Moral Sentiments*, was about the ability of humans to act out of empathy and altruism. Had he known that we would be measuring impact in the twenty-first century, he might well have combined his two books into one, and written about impact as the invisible *heart* of markets that guides their invisible hand.

Chapter 1

THE IMPACT REVOLUTION: RISK-RETURN-IMPACT

We must shift impact to the center of our consciousness

We cannot change the world by throwing more money at old concepts that no longer work – we need new concepts and approaches. New words are coined to capture new ideas, which is as true of economics as in the world of scientific discovery.

What does impact mean? It was in 2007, at a meeting hosted by the Rockefeller Foundation at its Bellagio Center in Italy, that 'impact investing' was coined as a term to replace 'social investment'. In its simplest terms, impact is the measure of an action's benefit to people and the planet. It goes beyond minimizing harmful outcomes to actively creating good ones by creating positive impact. It has social and environmental dimensions.

'Social impact' refers to the improvement in the well-being of individuals and communities, and the enhancement in their ability to lead productive lives.[1] It represents genuine social progress: educating the young, feeding the hungry, healing the sick, creating employment and providing livelihoods for the poor.

'Environmental impact' is just what it sounds like – the positive consequences that business activity and investment have on our planet. Put simply, are we preserving the planet and passing it on to future generations, so they can benefit from it and do the same?

> Impact needs to be brought to the heart of our society and take its place at the center of our economic system

Impact needs to be brought to the heart of our society and take its place at the center of our economic system. Our current system encourages decisions that are based on how to make as much money as possible with the lowest level of risk; we need to shift to a system that encourages making as much money as possible but in a way that is consistent with achieving the highest impact and with the lowest level of risk.

Impact must become ingrained in our society's DNA, part of a triple helix of risk–return–impact that influences every decision we make regarding consumption, employment, business and investment. It needs to become a driving force of our economy.

When we follow this new model, the social and environmental benefits of our decisions become central to our thinking rather than a mere afterthought. But to channel this new way of thinking into social and environmental improvement, we need to be able to measure impact dependably.

Though we take the prevailing model of risk and return for granted, it wasn't always the dominant model. Up until the twentieth century, business owners and investors only measured how much money they stood to make when deciding how to allocate capital. It wasn't until the second half of the twentieth century that the measurement of 'risk' was formally introduced and that it became natural to quantify risk and look at its relationship with return.

Risk is defined as the likelihood of adverse outcomes that could cost investors money. It sounds like an indefinable concept, and it used to be considered unmeasurable, but the academic community eventually found ways to standardize its measurement across all forms of investment; by the end of the twentieth century, everyone was talking about and measuring it in the same way.

The measurement of risk has had profound implications for the investment community. It introduced new theories like portfolio diversification, which gave rise to new asset classes that came with a higher level of risk, but also disproportionately improved returns. These new asset classes included venture capital, which funded the Tech Revolution, private equity and hedge funds. It also allowed new investment themes to take hold, like investment in emerging markets, which funded globalization.

If we fast-forward to the present day, we see that the same revolution that risk brought is now being brought by impact. Investments are increasingly examined for their positive and negative impact, and investors and businesses are becoming interested in factoring impact into their decision-making. Is it harder to measure than risk? Not at all – in fact, one can argue that it is easier. All over the world, people are developing methods to measure it.

The Impact Revolution promises to be just as world-changing as the Industrial Revolution or the more recent revolution in tech. It is a peaceful movement started by young consumers and entrepreneurs, who are disrupting the prevailing business models once again, but this time in order to improve lives, reduce inequality and improve the planet.

The Tech Revolution

It has been amazing to see how, within just a few decades of my life, new tech companies have overtaken giants that long dominated their field. Once-obscure start-ups such as Amazon, Apple, Google and Facebook have rocketed to the top 30 most valuable companies in the world in just 30 years.[2] We all know the stories of entrepreneurs who through their talent and drive have come up with new ways to solve old problems, pioneered invaluable new technologies and reshaped our modern world.

Of course, breakthroughs like this don't occur in a vacuum; one of the key factors that gave rise to the scale and speed of the Tech Revolution was the ready flow of venture capital investment, now a sector worth $1 trillion. If you told someone you worked in 'venture capital' 50 years ago, you would have been met with a blank stare.

Invented after the Second World War, venture capital gained a foothold in Silicon Valley in the 1970s and 1980s, and spread globally as the idea of investing in small, high-growth tech companies took off. Beyond their technical ingenuity, the skill of those early entrepreneurs lay in convincing investors there was money to be made by breathing life into their visions. Investors evaluate success based on profit, balancing the threat of risk and the potential for return. When they decided to invest in those early-stage tech companies, they were taking a leap of faith.

In the early 1980s, I was one such investor. The firm I co-founded, Apax Partners, invested in nearly 500 pioneering start-ups, each of which was intent on making an indelible mark on its field. Our investments included PPL Therapeutics, the company responsible for Dolly, the world's first cloned sheep, Apple and AOL.

One of the main reasons I became a venture capitalist was my feeling that I could make a positive impact on society while also doing well financially. Apax Partners backed hundreds of entrepreneurs who enriched themselves, as well as the people working with them and their communities. They created many thousands of jobs in new fields ranging from technology to consumer products and media. I believed that providing new sources of revenue and jobs to improve people's lives would elevate society as a whole.

However, as the years passed, I could see that the gap between rich and poor was widening. Some companies ended up doing more harm than good, and things got worse rather than better for many people at the bottom of the social pyramid. In the UK, even with the extension of the welfare state providing a safety net, poverty is still a huge challenge, and economic opportunity for the needy failed to expand meaningfully. The story is similar for the rest of the world. Although 60 million jobs were created in the new tech sector in the US, social and economic inequality continued to spread.

Part of the problem was due to supply and demand. The new skills required for tech jobs depended on higher-level education and so were in short supply. Firms competing for the talent drove tech salaries upwards, just as salaries in low-growth sectors were shrinking. The confluence of globalization, new technology that replaced workers and the flow of equity capital and cheap debt raised financial returns for the 1 per cent, while competition for qualified talent contributed to the perfect storm for making the rich richer and the poor poorer.

By 2000, it was clear that this model was failing society. The Tech Revolution had created incredible wealth and many social benefits, but huge social and environmental problems continued to plague our world, some of which had been made even worse. The relentless consumption of our natural resources raised global temperatures, leading to the loss of wildlife, deadly wildfires, flooding and the destruction of the biodiversity on which our existence depends.

If we do not fix these problems, the results could be catastrophic, so we need a new revolution in our thinking. We need new solutions that address both our social and environmental challenges – two streams that are now converging, as climate change leads to forced migration. But where will we find our bold solutions? If neither governments nor the private sector have been able to bring the urgently needed improvement at scale, perhaps the answer lies in changing our economic system.

The Birth of Impact

I began to realize that we needed a system that aligned the interests of business, investors and entrepreneurs with those of government, non-profit organizations, philanthropists and impact enterprises and drove them to work together to improve lives and the environment. But what could that look like? The answer turned out to be very simple: social initiatives needed to be connected to investment, which would enable entrepreneurs to finance purpose-driven businesses and charitable organizations. It would allow us to harness entrepreneurial talent and innovation to tackle old problems in new ways.

> When faced with huge social or environmental challenges, we must adjust our approach to investment in order to tackle them

Just as tech entrepreneurs were able to bring about change with the help of investment capital, impact entrepreneurs can make progress in overcoming the most pressing issues of our time. When faced with huge social or environmental challenges, we must adjust our approach to investment in order to tackle them. Investment is the fuel of our economic system, and in order to appeal to investors, it is helpful to start by viewing the world through their lens. This means focusing on profit and impact, evaluating success based on measurable results.

Reframing a social challenge as a chance to invest in our communities is more than a handy metaphor; it can deliver attractive financial returns and capture the interest of those who might otherwise focus their talent and investment on just making money.

In 2002, together with Philip Newborough, a former Apax colleague, and Michele Giddens, my right hand at the Social Investment Taskforce, I co-founded Bridges Fund Management to channel venture capital into the poorest parts of the UK. It was a simple idea: we would back businesses that were located in the poorest 25 per cent of Britain in order to improve the lives of the UK's most vulnerable populations. We wanted to make an impact through investment, so we thought like investors and set out to find a way to deliver measurable impact, alongside a 10–12 per cent annual financial return.

Eighteen years on, Bridges has raised over a billion pounds and delivered an average net annual return of 17 per cent. Just as importantly, it has done so while achieving significant impact; in 2017 alone, it delivered 1.3 million hours of quality care, provided healthcare services to 40,000 people, averted more than 30,000 tons of carbon emissions, directly supported over 2,600 jobs and helped over 2,600 children achieve better educational outcomes.[3] Through our investments, we have helped to scale some of the best impact businesses in the country.

The UK government backed Bridges' first fund with a £20 million ($26.6 million) investment, making it easier to attract private sector investment. It helped with another important social initiative in 2008, following the recommendations of the 'Commission on Unclaimed Assets', which I had set up three years earlier. The Labour government introduced legislation to direct money that was lying in unclaimed bank accounts[4] to flow to three social purposes: the establishment of a social investment bank, which the Social Investment Task Force had advocated in 2000, as well as youth and financial inclusion.

Four years later, £400 million ($532 million) of this money, supplemented by a further £200 million ($266 million) from the UK's four major banks, was used to establish Big Society Capital (BSC): the world's first 'social investment bank'. It was launched by David Cameron at the London Stock Exchange in April 2012. Since then, BSC has brought a significant boost to investment in charitable organizations, transforming their ability to scale and innovate.

Impact in Action

Encouraged by our early successes, in 2007 I created the UK's first social investment advisory firm, Social Finance, with the help of the philanthropists David Blood, Lord (Stanley) Fink, Sigrid Rausing and Philip Hulme. Our core mission was to invent ways of connecting social entrepreneurs with investment capital.

We set about recruiting talented young people from the financial and social sectors, and by the end of the third year our team had grown to 18 people, working under the chairmanship of Bernard Horn (formerly a director of NatWest Bank), with David Hutchison (formerly Head of UK Investment Banking at Dresdner Kleinwort) as our CEO.

Late in 2009, two members of the team, Toby Eccles and Emily Bolton, came to my office to talk about ways to reduce prisoner reoffending rates. Across the world, the statistics were jaw-dropping: as many as 60 per cent of young prisoners returned to prison within 18 months of their release.[5] This statistic had a ripple effect of negative consequences. Just imagine the human misery that could be avoided, the families reunited and the crime rates reduced, not to mention the savings for government, if we could somehow reduce that number.

Toby and Emily suggested that we tie the reduction in the reoffending rate to a financial return for investors, paying a return according to the social success that was achieved. In simple terms, investors would be paid for the increase in the number of prisoners who did not reoffend. This was a groundbreaking new idea.

I was inspired by the way in which venture capital had brought investors to fund the growth of start-ups. Working with Toby, Emily and David Hutchison, we designed the social impact bond as an investment instrument that would be capable of bringing investment to charitable social delivery organizations.

Armed with our proposal, which set out how the SIB worked, we went to meet Jack Straw, the Secretary of State for Justice. We offered to raise several million pounds from investors to fund charitable organizations that were already helping prisoners, if the Ministry of Justice would agree to pay investors back according to the increase in the number of prisoners that did not return to jail. The aim was to harness the profit-driven ingenuity of social entrepreneurs and the capital of investors in solving an unrelenting social problem.

When Jack Straw heard the idea, he banged the table, smiled and said to his officials, 'I know we're not supposed to do anything for the first time, but we're going to do *this*!' But how could preventing crime be a good investment? Well, crime is extraordinarily costly – governments spend millions every year fighting it and putting people in jail, not to mention housing and feeding prisoners once they are inside. If our effort helped the government save money, both investors and the organizations they funded could pocket a fraction of the money saved. Lives would improve, governments would save money and investors would make a reasonable profit. It was a win-win-win situation.

Viewing social challenges from the perspective of both delivery organizations and investors brought us to design the social impact bond (SIB) as a tool that helps social entrepreneurs accelerate social progress through the use of private investment.

One of the first people to realize the importance of the SIB was Prince Charles. Shortly after the announcement of the Peterborough SIB, I received a handwritten letter from him, welcoming the arrival of our SIB and hailing its potential to fund charitable organizations that would tackle social issues close to his heart. Coming from such a dedicated philanthropist, his words provided great encouragement for our endeavor.

The Social Impact Bond

Social impact bonds involve three key players: outcome payers, social service providers (these are generally non-profit organizations, but they can also be purpose-driven businesses) and investors. A financial advisor like Social Finance may help design and implement SIB transactions, and an independent evaluator verifies the outcomes achieved, rather as an auditor would.

The SIB, which is known as a PFS (Pay for Success) in the United States, an SBB (Social Benefit Bond) in Australia and a Social Impact Contract in France, is not a 'bond' in the traditional sense. In essence, it is an outcome-based contract for services between an 'outcome payer' who commissions a purpose-driven delivery organization to achieve a particular social outcome. A socially motivated investor then provides the funding to deliver the services, which eliminates the commissioner's financial risk.

If results do not meet the targets set in the contract, the investor loses their money, having effectively made a philanthropic donation. If, on the other hand, the targets are met, the investor receives their investment back, with a return that rises with the extent of the outcomes achieved.

The outcome funder is the party that pays back the investors, having achieved the social improvement it seeks from the program. Usually a government but sometimes an official aid organization or a philanthropic foundation, they will work with the financial intermediary or the delivery organization directly to set objectives, timelines and payment levels, and they will only pay investors when the predetermined positive outcomes are achieved.

This system has several advantages for the service provider – non-profits or purpose-driven businesses that deliver a social service or intervention. It fortifies them with large amounts of funding upfront and gives them the flexibility to run their interventions according to what will achieve the best outcomes, allowing them to experiment and innovate.

Historically, service providers that get their funding from philanthropy are evaluated on measures that center around their activities. To gauge success, philanthropists might look at activities such as the number of prisoners they enroll in a rehabilitation program, or inputs such as the hours spent educating prisoners.

In contrast, a focus on outcomes would look at the reduction in the reoffending rate, which is at the end of the day more important than how many prisoners were enrolled in the program. This shift in evaluation motivates service providers to focus on core objectives and collaborate in new and efficient ways in order to achieve them.

When we set out at Social Finance to reduce reoffending rates in the UK, we created the social impact bond described above. Our investors were 17 charitable foundations, including the Esmée Fairbairn Foundation in the UK and the Rockefeller Foundation in the US.

We met with officials from the British government and reached a deal: we would raise £5 million ($6.7 million) to finance charitable service providers that had been working with prisoners at the Peterborough jail. If, after five to seven years, we had failed to reduce the reoffending rate by 7.5

per cent relative to a control group of released prisoners, no money would return to the investors. However, if the rate of reoffending fell by 7.5 per cent or more, the government would repay the initial investment, in addition to a rate of interest that would rise according to the reduction achieved. The crux of this initiative was that the government would be paying out only 30–50 per cent of the money that would be saved on law courts and prisons: after paying back the investors, they would still come in under budget. Meanwhile, the investing foundations could reinvest their money in other impact-generating initiatives, and the charitable service providers would continue to receive funding to support their work.

The Peterborough SIB achieved a 9.7 per cent reduction in the number of convictions, and paid investors 3.1 per cent a year on top of their capital. Lives were improved, government reduced the burden on law courts and prisons, and investors saw a return – the SIB represented a new way of thinking about the role of finance in social progress.

Some might suggest that philanthropists are already funding this kind of work, but this is only partly true. Some of the charitable foundations we worked with were already financing prisoner rehabilitation, but we grouped them together and pooled their capital into a single initiative that was focused on hitting a concrete and measurable goal, with more money going to service providers who were doing valuable work with prisoners but lacked the money to operate at scale.

Our work also united those service providers under one umbrella, coordinating their efforts. The final thing we achieved was helping those charitable foundations, our investors, earn back the money they spent, with some extra on top, so they could reinvest it. This model, if widely adopted, has huge potential for anyone seeking to tackle social issues, whether in the non-profit sector, business or government.

The implications for the social sector are huge. In the UK alone, between 800,000 and one million people work in the non-profit sector, while UK charitable foundations hold around £100 billion ($133 billion) of assets.[6] In Europe, 11 million people work in non-profit organizations. In the USA, 9–10 million people work for over 1.7 million charitable organizations, while US foundations hold assets of $850 billion.[7] But despite these significant resources, it is striking that charitable organizations invariably tend to be short of money and that few achieve scale.

SIBs Go Global

The success of the first SIB demonstrated that private investment *could* be mobilized to tackle even the most persistent social problems. As former British prime minister Gordon Brown said, the Peterborough SIB became 'the guiding light for hundreds of millions of dollars in investment in social reform'.[8] And it has indeed led to the development of SIBs all around the world.

In the USA, it was my close colleague Tracy Palandjian who spearheaded the SIB movement. I met her shortly after the creation of Social Finance in the UK, when I was at an event to celebrate the centenary of Harvard Business School. I shared the stage with former US Treasury Secretary Larry Summers and Professor Michael Porter, and we discussed the role of private investment in tackling social issues.

Tracy, a Harvard Business School graduate herself, was in the audience, and we discussed insights from the panel. Three years later, after the launch of the Peterborough SIB, I was keen for Social Finance to expand into the USA, where financial innovation takes root faster than anywhere else in the world. I called Tracy and invited her to join David Blood and myself in co-founding Social Finance US, which we did at the beginning of 2011. Under her leadership, the USA has become the market where SIBs have scaled the most, attracting more investment than anywhere else in the world.

Confidence in the SIB continued to grow, and in 2016 the UK government demonstrated its commitment by launching the first-ever public fund to pay for the outcomes of SIB programs. Known as an Outcome Fund, the £80 million ($106.4 million) Life Chances Fund (LCF) seeks to help the most disadvantaged in society.[9] The LCF pays for around 20 per cent of the outcome payments due, while local government commissioners pay the other 80 per cent.

So what exactly do we mean by an Outcome Fund? If we return to the Peterborough SIB, the money paid back to investors following a successful intervention would be funded by an Outcome Fund instead of the Ministry of Justice. Philanthropists can either create them or participate in independent Outcome Funds, which are set up by others, to increase the capability of the organizations they support to achieve a specific mission. For example, the GSG is mobilizing two Education Outcomes Funds, each of $1 billion, to improve educational attainment levels. One of them is in Africa and the Middle East, in partnership with the Education Commission chaired by Gordon Brown, and the other is in India, alongside the smaller Outcome Fund recently launched by the British Asian Trust.

There are now more than 190 social and development impact bonds across 32 countries, which between them tackle a dozen different social issues. DIBs, which focus on emerging countries, have the same structure as SIBs, but their outcome payers are usually made up of a combination of governments, aid organizations and philanthropists. SIBs and DIBs are powerful because they reframe social and environmental challenges as investment opportunities. They represent a compelling new asset category for investors, as their returns do not fluctuate with stock markets or interest rates. For outcome payers, they represent an outcomes-based contract that delivers better results and provides greater transparency on what works and what doesn't than a conventional contract that pays for activities.

SIBs and DIBs are the purest expression of risk–return–impact at work. They are part of a general shift, which is already under way, to a system whose model of decision-making introduces this new mindset of risk–return–impact, rather than risk–return. They also make us realize that the impact of social interventions can actually be measured.

This realization is now spreading to the broader understanding that impact can be measured and compared across companies, transforming all decision-making that relates to them. Such comparison will motivate every decision we make regarding consumption, employment and investment, guiding companies to deliver positive impact. That is what the Impact Revolution is about.

Measuring and Valuing Impact

Measuring impact has the power to galvanize action. Take what happened in 2008, when the US embassy in Beijing decided to place sensors on its roof, so that it could advise its employees when pollution levels were so high that they should stay indoors. The sensors automatically tweeted data every hour, which put pressure on the Chinese government, since its own published data tended to understate the real levels. By 2013, the Chinese government acknowledged the severity of air pollution in the city, and pledged hundreds of billions of dollars to reduce it.[10]

To change the behavior of investors and companies, it is essential that we measure companies' positive and negative social and environmental impacts in a way that is easily understood by everyone. Former US vice-president Al Gore, among others, has for decades advocated the measurement of 'externalities' created by companies, as part of his fight against climate change. But no dependable way of measuring and integrating the impact of companies has emerged to date.

If we regard impact investing as our rocket ship to social change, impact measurement is our navigation system. It will lead to change and the establishment of new norms. However, to achieve the widespread use of impact measurement, we need to completely rethink how we consider impact

– for too long, we have assessed it in ways that are imprecise and inconsistent.

There are currently over 150 different impact assessment efforts across the world,[11] each approaching impact measurement from a different perspective. Even traditional accountancy firms have started to pay more attention to sustainability issues and what they mean for business. There is a real need for a standardized way of defining, measuring and valuing impact in a similar way we do with profit.

> If we regard impact investing as our rocket ship to social change, impact measurement is our navigation system

One of the most promising efforts to galvanize such an approach to impact measurement is the Impact-Weighted Accounts Initiative (IWAI). This is a joint initiative between The Global Steering Group for Impact Investment (GSG), the driver of the impact movement across the world; the Impact Management Project (IMP), a body of two thousand practitioners, set up by Bridges Fund Management in 2016 under the leadership of Clara Barby, which is working towards a consensus on how to measure impact; and Harvard Business School.

The CEO of the IWAI is George Serafeim, an inspiring Harvard Business School professor of accounting. I chair its Leadership Council with Clara Barby as the vice-chair. The IWAI brings together academics and figures from the worlds of business, investment and accounting. Its novel approach involves integrating the impact a company creates into its regular financial accounts. The goal is to create a framework through which the impact created by a company directly affects its value, in a similar way that its profit does. We will explore how this works in Chapter 4.

A major benefit of impact measurement is that it prevents the moral hazard of 'impact washing', when a business falsely claims to engage in socially beneficial work. For some businesses today, such claims are little more than a marketing ploy. In order to authentically integrate impact into business and investment decision-making, impact must be dependably measured.

The Role of Government

Only governments have the power to require businesses and investors to measure and report on the impact of their activities according to uniform metrics. In the prisoner reoffending initiative discussed earlier in this chapter, the UK government measured the success of the program in terms of public savings.

To help make this way of thinking commonplace, the UK government published its Unit Cost Database in 2014, which lists the estimated cost to the country of more than 600 issues, ranging from crime and unemployment to homelessness. These estimates allow the reliable quantification of at least part of the benefit that an impact investment achieves and are used by local commissioners, charitable organizations and social enterprises to inform outcome-based contracting and the terms offered by social impact bonds.[12]

Some governments, like Portugal's, have followed the UK's lead, and some independent efforts are being made in parallel to quantify the cost of social issues globally. One such effort is the Global Value Exchange, a crowd-sourced database of over 30,000 impact measurement metrics that offers valuations in a similar way to the Unit Cost Database.[13] For example, you can find out the annual cost of a homeless person who is out of work in the UK based on the benefits payments they receive, their lost income tax and national insurance payments, and their lost economic output.[14]

Our priority now should be to work towards standardized metrics for each social area. This will enable us to make comparisons between the impact of different interventions. The aim is to go beyond measuring a single impact to measuring all significant impacts created by organizations and initiatives.

Whether public or private, all organizations make an impact; it is time to measure this reliably, value it explicitly and demand better of decision-makers across the globe. Once we measure and value impact properly, investors and businesses will factor impact into their decisions as second nature; eventually, *all* investing will be impact investing.

The Way Forward

The shift to optimizing risk–return–impact, which is led by entrepreneurs and investors, will have a much-needed and transformative effect on the flow of capital in our economies.

There is no other way to cope with the scale and severity of social and environmental issues other than to attract investment capital from the $200 trillion of investable assets in our financial system.

Evidence of the Impact Revolution is already clear in the growing recognition among consumers, employees and investors that businesses have an obligation to serve not just their shareholders, but their customers, employees, communities and the environment; that impact needs to be a crucial part of everyone's mission. We are at a point that is equivalent to the moment when the idea of risk gave rise to venture capital and investment in tech companies, but this time it is the idea of impact that is giving rise to impact investing and changing the world of investment.

This change is reflected in the over 2,600 investors from more than 70 countries[15] who have signed up $90 trillion of assets to the Principles of Responsible Investment (PRIs), which encourage signatories to invest responsibly and create a more sustainable global financial system. Signatories of the PRIs, which were established in 2006 by the United Nations, agree to take social and environmental considerations into account when making investment decisions. It is also reflected in the $31 trillion that is already invested in targeting environmental, social and governance improvement.

It is captured in the letter which Larry Fink, the CEO of Blackrock, the world's largest asset manager, published in 2018 stating that 'society is demanding that companies, both public and private, serve a social purpose' and that 'to prosper over time, every company must not only deliver financial performance, but also show how it makes a positive contribution to society.'[16]

This change can have hugely positive consequences for how we invest, how we do business and how we spend our money. It will shift our economies to deliver a transformative impact on billions of lives and the planet. The Impact Revolution leads consumers, entrepreneurs, investors, businesses, philanthropists and governments to create tangible and measurable impact. It brings risk–return–impact to the center of our decision-making to change our whole economic system.

Our current economic system generates negative impact and relies on government and philanthropy to solve the problems it creates. Our system is more than two centuries old. Our problems have changed, so our response must change too.

An evolution in our thinking, which brings us the triple helix of risk–return–impact, is creating a revolution in our means, through impact investing, to meet the challenges we face. The following chapters will examine what entrepreneurs, investors, businesses, philanthropists and governments are already doing, and what they need to do next to accelerate the advance of the Impact Revolution.

Chapter 2

THE AGE OF IMPACT ENTREPRENEURSHIP

It is possible to do well and do good at the same time

You will likely have heard people say that the best thing to do is make as much money as possible without worrying about doing good, before becoming a generous philanthropist and giving lots of money away to good causes. This has long been the traditional model, but things are changing – impact entrepreneurship shows there is a better model for how to lead our lives, as well as showing that it is possible for businesses to do good and make money at the same time. So what does this mean for the budding entrepreneur who dreams of launching a business that makes the world a better place, but doesn't know where to start?

Some of our most thrilling social innovations have begun with more questions than answers. Questions like 'How can I use my skill set for good?', 'How can I generate profit and impact at the same time?' and 'Am I ready to start a venture of my own?'

I started the business that became Apax Partners at the age of 26. When friends suggested that it might be wiser to gain more experience first, I'd say, 'You can't learn to swim by exercising on the beach.' The best thing to do at that time, in the new field of venture capital, was to dive in, learn fast and gain experience ahead of others. The same is true of impact ventures today.

Young entrepreneurs are inventing impact-driven businesses that serve customers better, improve lives and help to preserve our planet. As with the Tech Revolution, it is ambitious young companies that are leading the way. Inspired by the idea of risk–return–impact and backed by new sources of funding, young people today, whether they are in jobs, earning their MBAs

Impact entrepreneurship shows there is a better model for how to lead our lives

or working in research labs in Silicon Valley, are rejecting the harmful practices of their predecessors and committing to impact. The dream of building a unicorn (a start-up worth over $1 billion) is being re-evaluated. Why should young entrepreneurs not set their sights on building an 'impact unicorn' that is worth $1 billion and improves the lives of one billion people at the same time?

There are many reasons why the profit-with-purpose model of impact ventures is an increasingly sensible business decision, in addition to a compelling moral one. For one thing, being able to supply underserved populations with products and services allows businesses to tap into huge demand, which in turn creates the opportunity to grow more quickly than companies that serve mainstream markets at higher prices.

Socially conscious companies also avoid the risk of punitive taxes that governments might impose in the future, such as a carbon tax. Furthermore, consumers, employees and investors are increasingly shunning harmful companies and embracing those that make a positive difference. I have heard prominent figures from the business world say that you cannot ride two horses, making money and doing good, at the same time. The examples in this chapter will show that, in fact, we can harness these two horses, doing good and doing well. Starting an impact venture is a reliable way to be more successful.

Many of us are familiar with the impact pioneers who have blazed a trail: companies like Patagonia, TOMS shoes and Warby Parker. This chapter will reveal some of the companies that have more recently brought impact innovation in different ways, in sectors ranging from technology and healthcare to agriculture and consumer goods. Many are helped by new legal structures, certification and mentoring organizations that support their impact-driven entrepreneurial efforts around the globe.

> We can harness these two horses, doing good and doing well

Taken together, the following ventures show how impact can transform every sector of our economy. They demonstrate that a trade-off between financial and social returns is not necessary; in fact, these companies often show returns not in spite of impact but *because* of it. If you are asking how to do well while also doing good, these stories may inspire you to start now. Many of these ventures start with an entrepreneur finding new uses for the latest technology and adapting it to fit the requirements of those in need. That is what Zipline has done.

Life-Saving Drones to the Rescue

On 21 December 2016, an order arrived at a drone base near Kigali in Rwanda. Upon receiving the message, a technician strapped in the consignment and prepared a drone for launch; within minutes it was heading toward its target, a district hospital a six-minute flight away.

Inside the hospital lay a motionless two-year-old girl called Ghislane, who had been ravaged by an acute form of malaria. Within minutes of being summoned, the drone hovered near the hospital entrance and dropped a red box containing two units of refrigerated blood that floated to the ground on a paper parachute. A year earlier, this same hospital would have had to dispatch a car to fetch the blood from a bank located a three-hour round-trip away, a delay that might have ended this young girl's life.[1]

This story can be tied back to the story of Keller Rinaudo, a professional robotics entrepreneur who, after starting a toy robot company at the age of 23, challenged himself to focus his business 'on things that would have a profound impact on people's lives'.[2] The difficulty was he didn't know how to do it or what the impact should be. 'There was a rough patch where people were questioning my sanity,' he now says.[3]

Rinaudo and his co-founders scoured the globe for problems they thought could be solved using their skillset. In robotics, 'You want boring ... you want repetitive. We looked for places where logistics breaks down, because that's a good place to start,' he says.[4] He decided to tackle the logistics of delivering essential medical products, such as life-saving blood for a transfusion. Managing storage and inventory was tricky, which led to oversupply in some geographies, undersupply in others and waste from spoiled products. When the blood was needed, the patient didn't have time to spare. He and his team knew they could improve delivery efficiency and reduce waste with robotics: they would create a distribution center to store blood and fly drones to deliver it to precisely where it was needed. To sustain the company, they would charge for each delivery.

Rinaudo called his company Zipline and chose to pilot its technology and logistics system in Rwanda; the country's mountainous and muddy roads were at times impassable and infrastructure was lacking, but the government was 'filled with young people who make decisions fast and are willing to take risks'.[5]

According to Rinaudo, using Zipline saved the Rwandan government money, while also saving precious time and lives, and the company's drones could serve 80 per cent of Rwanda's population with just two distribution centers.[6] By the end of 2018, the company had delivered 15,000 units of blood and had plans to expand to Tanzania and the US and to pursue the delivery of other medical supplies, such as vaccines for babies and emergency medicines.

Thinking forward, the company is dedicated to increasing the capacity of its drones through improved technology.

In April 2018, Zipline unveiled a new model that 'flies farther, faster and with more cargo than was ever before possible – even in high altitude, heavy wind, or rain'.[7] The company's long-term mission is 'to build instant delivery for the planet, allowing on-demand delivery of medicines and other products at low cost without using a drop of gasoline'.[8]

In May 2019, Zipline secured $190 million in funding from US venture capitalists and achieved a $1.2 billion valuation.[9] It announced that it would expand across Africa, the Americas, South Asia and Southeast Asia, with the goal of serving 700 million people in the next five years.[10] 'Zipline wants to establish a new model for success in Silicon Valley,' Rinaudo said, 'by showing the world that the right technology company with the right mission and the best team can help improve the lives of every person on the planet.'[11]

While Rinaudo and his team have reimagined drone technology, another entrepreneurial tech-for-good venture, OrCam in Israel, has repurposed advanced technology in artificial intelligence, initially developed to guide driverless cars, to help the 39 million blind and the 250 million visually impaired people around the world.

From Driverless Cars to Helping the Blind

In 2016, 27-year-old Luke Hines was able to imagine going to college for the first time.[12] In 2018, war veteran Scotty Smiley was finally able to read with his three sons.[13] In 2019, Naim Bassa was empowered to cast his vote for the first time without someone having to accompany him.[14] These three people were all visually impaired but had access to OrCam's assistive technology, which uses a camera, computing, machine learning and deep networks to process visual information and relay it to users phonetically.

But the story of this wearable technology began in 1999, when co-founders Professor Amnon Shashua and Ziv Aviram started Mobileye, a technology company that uses cameras and artificial intelligence to replace the human eye in driverless cars.[15] Eighteen years later they sold the company to Intel for over $15 billion, the largest acquisition in Israel's history.[16]

At this point, Shashua began thinking of applying the technology he had invented to assist his aunt, whose vision was worsening.[17] He and Aviram co-founded OrCam in 2010 to help visually impaired people process their surroundings.

In 2017, Orcam released MyEye 2. Completely wireless and about the size of a finger, it could read printed text, recognize faces, products, barcodes and bank notes. When the wearer pointed toward any of these, the device would relay what it saw in their ear.

One user said that MyEye gave him the ability to 'pick up anything – a newspaper, a book, a menu – and you don't have to rely on other people. When letters come through the door, you can just read them without having to hassle anyone else.'[18]

By 2018, OrCam had raised over $130 million and was valued at $1 billion.[19] 'I think the potential for OrCam is even bigger than Mobileye,' said Aviram.[20] For someone like Lisa Hayes in Australia, who has been blind since birth, the Orcam product is miraculous. She said about the device, 'It has got to be the breakthrough of the twenty-first century as far as I'm concerned.'[21]

Impact entrepreneurs will ask themselves about the best way of helping the maximum number of people through their technology. Asking this question about OrCam's technology leads us in an interesting direction: why not apply these same products to help the 781 million *illiterate* adults around the world, as well? OrCam's potential market may thus extend to nearly 15 per cent of the world's population of 7.7 billion. Imagine the impact of this technology on the lives of more than one billion people, the economic contribution they might make to their countries and the impact on the world's economy. Impact thinking uncovers opportunities that we would otherwise miss.

Many other start-ups are developing businesses that aim to improve the lives of people around the globe who suffer from disabilities. The entrepreneurs leading these ventures are often driven, like Amnon Shahua, by a desire to help an individual dear to them.

One Word to Full Conversations

Brazilian entrepreneur Carlos Edmar Pereira had a daughter who was born with cerebral palsy in 2008 and unable to walk or speak. Desperate to improve her quality of life, Pereira taught himself to code and developed software to help individuals with diverse disabilities to communicate. 'I was obsessed all the time, on the computer, late at night to code this program for my daughter,' he said.[22]

Livox's dynamic software adapts to a person's physical and cognitive capabilities to help them interact in real time with those around them, such as families and teachers. 'For example, if they can't use their limbs, they can use their eyes,' said Pereira.[23] Using the front-facing camera on a tablet, he developed a capability that would allow users to interact with the tablet by moving their eyes. Moreover, Livox offered it at a fraction of the current cost – a Livox license costs $250, compared to roughly $17,000 for a typical device controlled by eye.[24] For those that can use their hands or even their toes, the Livox software uses intelligent algorithms that adjust to and compensate for a user's unique movements, whether they use their whole hand or multiple fingers to touch the screen, or even make involuntary taps.[25] One mother of an autistic child said that her daughter 'has gone from literally one word to having conversations with me with the device'.[26]

While Pereira was motivated to develop Livox to improve his daughter's life, he wants to ensure that he reaches the billion people with disabilities and helps them to live better lives as well. 'They are the group with the highest risk of social exclusion,' he said.[27] Many of Livox's licenses are sold to the Brazilian government. He sells them at discounted rates and they go to low-income families. He is eager to scale his business, especially to schools, hospitals and developing countries.[28]

Lending on the Back of a Cell-Phone

While the entrepreneurs leading OrCam, Livox and Zipline are building businesses that can achieve social impact through the use of information technology, Shivani Siroya, the Kenyan founder of Tala, is using fintech and data to provide credit to entrepreneurs who cannot obtain it from conventional banks.

The premise of Tala, a mobile lending platform that operates in India, Kenya, Mexico, the Philippines and Tanzania, is that not having a credit history doesn't mean that a person is not creditworthy. Rather than relying on the usual formal records such as bank statements, Tala makes use of the data that is already sitting on our mobile phones. A smartphone user can download the Tala mobile app, which scrapes over ten thousand data points from a user's device, including app usage, calls, texts and transactions.[29] Tala then predicts a person's likelihood that they will be able to repay a loan. For example, the company found that if a person's phone contacts are stored with first and last names, they have a higher chance of repaying.

'We can predict creditworthiness in about 20 seconds, based on data that's already sitting on a customer's device,' said Shivani Siroya,[30] Tala's founder, who grew up in India and started the company when in her late twenties in 2012. After they have been approved, customers receive money in their mobile wallet. 'We look at people by what they're doing in their daily lives, not some payment they might have missed three years ago,' she said.[31]

Loans are generally $10 to $500 and carry 11 to 15 per cent interest, due within 30 days.[32] As of 2019, the company had lent more than $1 billion to over 4 million people and had a repayment rate of 90 per cent.[33] This is a far cry from how the enterprise started, with Siroya lending her own money to 50 people or so in India, Ghana, Mali and Mexico.[34] Early on, her borrowers had a 30 per cent default rate, but as she gathered more data and was able to build a robust credit model, the default rate decreased to less than 10 per cent – better than a traditional credit bureau would predict.[35]

Clients tend to use the microloans as one might use a credit card: two-thirds take out loans for their business, while others use the credit for education, emergency travel, medical expenses or other personal needs. Grace, who sells clothing in Kenya, said, 'My customers usually don't pay for the clothes immediately, so I usually borrow to ensure I can go to the market and buy goods for sale as I wait for payment.'[36]

Siroya, who gained experience at UBS, Credit Suisse and Citi before she launched Tala, said of her early research of the microfinance sector, 'I started to realize that one of the major problems was how to get someone from the microfinance system into the formal credit system?'[37] To help micro-borrowers gain access to formal credit, she helps customers build a public record by reporting their repayment history to traditional credit bureaus. Shannon Yates, a data analytics lead at Tala said, 'We want to reinforce the concept that [customers] can leverage credit to benefit them in the long run, even if not immediately.'[38]

In the short term, Tala gives clients access to stable funds, decreasing anxiety and stress in their lives and those of their families. In the long term, Tala customers experience financial growth, access to traditional banks and enhanced financial literacy,[39] things which are key not only to allowing entrepreneurs to thrive, but also to growing local economies.

Tala had raised more than $105 million over three rounds of funding by April 2018,[40] with PayPal joining the list of investors that October.[41] On the day Tala announced its $65 million third round, Siroya was asked where she saw the company in five years' time. She responded, 'We'll have proved that it's possible to succeed by doing things differently – that mission and profit are not a zero-sum game, that you can be for both of these things and still win.'[42]

Fintech is undoubtedly a powerful way for impact entrepreneurs to improve lives. So is biotechnology, which is remastering very traditional fields, such as agriculture, to improve the livelihood of farmers and feed the world.

Seeding Innovation to Feed the World

With 7.5 billion mouths to feed and the Earth's climate changing before our eyes, agriculture is arguably the sector on the planet that is capable of delivering the most impact. There's work to be done: studies have shown that we need to increase crop production by between 25 and 70 per cent by 2050 in order to feed ourselves.[43]

Indigo Agriculture, a Massachusetts-based start-up, is leveraging microbiology not just to increase crop yields but also to reduce usage of agricultural chemicals. The company's founders were inspired by research on the human gut microbiome. The communities of microbes inside us are said to ward off harm and contribute to our health,[44] and Geoffrey von Maltzahn applied this thinking to agriculture. After earning a PhD in biomedical engineering from MIT, he co-founded Indigo in 2016 when he was in his mid-thirties. As he said, 'The microbiome might be both more powerful and a more natural means of influencing the traits and the properties of agricultural crops.'[45] In other words, thriving microbiomes may safeguard crops from disease, drought and pests better than our current practices.

Indigo's model entails identifying the effective microbes in healthy crops, and adding them to seeds which are sold to farmers. These seeds are thus primed to grow into highly resilient and productive plants that can flourish without the use of synthetic chemicals. Indigo reported increased crop yields of between 6 and 14 per cent from their cotton, soybeans, corn, rice and wheat seeds.[46]

By 2019, Indigo had raised $650 million via half a dozen funding rounds and was valued at $3 billion.[47] In addition to enormous investment into the science behind the human microbiome, the company has been able to take advantage of several converging technological advances, including improvements in DNA sequencing technology, computational tools and connectivity.[48] As von Maltzahn said, 'Anybody with a cell phone and a pair of scissors can give us a plant sample, and we'll know the GPS location, the time of day, the weather history of that site, infer the stress profile that it was under, infer its fitness from a photograph and then be able to figure out the plant species and sequence the microbiome at an ever-increasingly diminished cost.'[49]

Not all impact ventures use technology in this way. The founders of Andela are targeting major challenges without relying on technological innovation; instead, they are innovating through their business model to improve the ability of people in emerging countries to secure higher paying jobs.

Tapping Brilliance Across the World

In 2014, Tolulope Komolafe, a Nigerian in her mid-twenties, was tutoring students in math and earning $25 a month.[50] She had graduated with a degree in computer science[51] but had become part of the estimated 40 per cent of the country's population who was either unemployed or underemployed.[52]

When Komolafe saw an opportunity at a start-up in Lagos that would pay her while training her to be a software developer for global companies, she thought at first that she was being scammed and that it was 'too good to be true'.[53] But the opportunity – posted by Andela, a tech company and global talent accelerator – was legitimate.

Komolafe distinguished herself enough from the other 2,500 applicants to become one of the start-up's second cohort of fellows – a group of 20 people.[54] She was soon enrolled in a coding bootcamp and in soft-skills training.[55] After a thousand hours of professional development, she was deemed qualified to work for Andela's clients[56] – firms that ranged from IBM to smaller companies like GitHub.[57]

Unlike outsourcing models typically associated with India and China that primarily compete on price, Komolafe and her colleagues at Andela were embedded into the client companies, some of which went as far as offering the Andela fellows equity stakes.[58] Everplans, an end-of-life planning platform that Komolafe worked for, invited her to an orientation in New York City, where she was able to meet colleagues with whom she had been working for months.[59] By 2016, Christina Sass, co-founder and president of Andela, was calling her the start-up's star developer.[60]

Andela got its start in 2013, when serial entrepreneur Iyinoluwa 'E' Aboyeji, a Nigerian in his early twenties, contacted Jeremy Johnson, an American education technology entrepreneur, for advice. Johnson soon agreed to become CEO of the new enterprise and brought Sass onboard.

The driving force behind the venture was the belief that brilliance is evenly distributed across the world, though opportunity is not. The team got to work seeking and developing brilliant minds into tech talent that would fill the gap in countries where the shortage and high cost of tech professionals are a hindrance to start-up growth.

Most of the Andela developers lived 'on campus' in subsidized housing during their fellowship immersion program.[61] 'The long-term goal is for them to be unleashed, to really spread and lead the spread of technology across the continent,' said Sass.[62] According to Sass, a quarter of them wanted to start their own companies,[63] while others might become tech leaders at existing companies, advisors to organizations or help Andela scale its model.[64]

Andela's business model – with a focus on workforce development, education and tech – and its longer-term goals of helping grow the African tech sector, had attracted the attention of highly sought-after investors. In 2015, AOL co-founder Steve Case and Omidyar were among those who participated in a funding round totaling $10 million to help Andela expand across the continent.[65]

A year later, Andela captured the eye of Facebook's Mark Zuckerberg and his wife Priscilla Chan, who led a $24-million second round of funding through their Chan Zuckerberg Initiative. In fact, Andela was CZI's first lead investment and they were accompanied by GV (formerly Google Ventures), Spark Capital, Omidyar Network, Learn Capital and CRE Venture Capital. Shortly after investing, Zuckerberg traveled to Lagos to visit the Andela office and meet the company's staff. Sass said in an interview, 'We said to all of our applicants, especially in the early days ... we are going to tell the entire world about the caliber of your talent. And in an instant, that just became incredibly real to them the second that [Mark Zuckerberg] walked in.'[66]

In 2017, the company raised $40 million in a third funding round led by CRE Venture Capital, one of the largest ever rounds in an Africa-based company to be led by an African venture firm. The new money would fund Andela's expansion into two more African countries and double its base of developers.[67]

By 2019, Andela had served more than 200 clients, attracted over 130,000 applications and selected 1,500 developers. As *The Economist* wrote, Andela 'demonstrates how pure brainpower can be exported from a snazzy office block in Lagos to sophisticated customers halfway around the world without going near an overcrowded port or broken railway line'.[68]

The same year, a fourth round of $100 million brought Andela's total funding to $180 million. The round was led by Generation Investment Management, the sustainability-focused investment firm founded by Al Gore and David Blood.[69]

As for Komolafe, she says her goal is to use her skills as a coder to make an impact. 'Long-term, I would want to join a team of people who are solving problems ... [like] child abuse,' she said. 'Every day, I think of how I can apply everything I know about tech to actually solving that problem.'[70]

Impact entrepreneurs are also able to build successful ventures by revolutionizing a traditional product. Revolution Foods in California and Nazid Impact Food in Israel do just that, by focusing on the health of schoolchildren in different parts of the world.

Giving Kids the Fuel for Success

Imagine that you're a child who wakes up hungry but without a dollar to your name. You get ready for school without breakfast. Your first meal of the day is in the school cafeteria at lunchtime, but by then your stomach is in knots. You wait in line and something barely recognizable is slopped onto your tray. You can barely bring yourself to take a bite, but then lunchtime is over.

This is what it's like for many students, even in developed countries, but they're still expected to concentrate during classes and perform normally.[71] In the US, more than 13 million children arrive at school hungry. The quality of food in schools can be poor, and unappetizing presentation can lead to children choosing junk food over a hot school lunch or even going hungry. As one *New York Times* writer put it, 'standard cafeteria fare is doing little to curb the nation's rising rate of childhood obesity and might even be contributing to it.'[72]

Hungry children are challenged to perform academically, while hunger inhibits concentration and can lead to behavioral problems.[73] With children in the US consuming as much as half their calories in school,[74] ensuring access to high-quality food should be a priority, but budgets make it a challenge.

Fortunately for American schoolchildren, Kirsten Saenz Tobey and Kristin Groos Richmond created Revolution Foods to encourage healthy eating at schools. The two met on the first day of their MBA program at the Haas School of Business at the University of California, Berkeley, and became close friends. Both had an education background and had lived abroad, and Groos Richmond had worked in finance.

During graduate school, the two developed a business plan to create 'meals with fresh ingredients at a manageable price'.[75] Tobey said, 'We spent a lot of time in class writing the business plan for the company and going out talking to students, teachers, school leaders and superintendents about what opportunities they saw for improving the quality of school food.'[76]

Upon graduation in 2006, they immediately began a pilot program in downtown Oakland, California, preparing 300 meals for children a day in a rented kitchen. The food was prepared fresh every day and was free of artificial colors, flavors, preservatives and sweeteners. They served hormone-free milk and meats and prioritized organic and locally grown ingredients – it was all what the women called 'real food'.[77]

The enterprise began serving mostly charter and low-income schools, but by 2012, Revolution Foods was serving 200,000 meals a day in 850 schools across 11 states, including Texas, New York and Louisiana,[78] at mostly public schools, where 80 per cent of children qualified for the free or reduced priced lunch program because of their household income.[79] 'That was really the founding premise of our company – making sure that the kids that qualify for free lunch at school could get just as high-quality food as the kids who can afford it,' said Tobey.[80]

Positive outcomes were wide-ranging. According to testimonials, the healthier food provided 'better concentration, less disciplinary action, less trips to the nurses [and] less absences', said Groos Richmond.[81]

In 2014, Steve Case invested $30 million through his Revolution Growth fund. 'The school lunch business is a $16-billion business in the US alone,' he said.[82] By 2015, the company had posted $80 million in revenue.[83] By 2019, it had raised nearly $130 million in funding[84] and had hit $150 million in revenue.[85] By this point it was serving over 2.5 million meals every week,[86] in 400 cities and towns across the US, including over 225,000 meals across New York and New Jersey alone.[87] 'Our ultimate goal is giving kids the fuel they need to set them up for success,' said Tobey.[88]

The power of impact entrepreneurship in providing healthier and tastier school meals knows no boundaries, and so it is that the enterprising innovation of Revolution Foods in the USA is also found on the other side of the world, within the Bedouin community of Israel.

Bedouins hold a unique cultural and historical identity and also form part of the most underserved section of Israeli society. Unemployment in their community is very high, at around 40 per cent, and the average wage of Bedouin workers is less than half the national average. Women face even greater barriers to fair and effective employment, as is often the case.

Ibrahim Nassara, an entrepreneur from a Bedouin town with the lowest socio-economic ranking, recognized that there was unmet need for healthy school meals in his community. He founded Nazid Impact Food in 2011, to improve the subsidized school meals that Bedouin children received at lunchtime. Starting with three women cooking 300 meals a day, Nazid now employs more than 100 people from the Bedouin community, who between them prepare over 20,000 meals every day for schools across Israel.

Nazid delivers impact in two ways. By providing healthy, tasty food, it improves the nourishment of underserved school children. At the same time, through employment that includes fair wages and benefits, Nazid improves the income of Bedouin families and also integrates Bedouin women into employment, allowing them to achieve personal and financial independence. The company's impact was recognized in 2019, when Nazid became the first Bedouin-led company to receive private equity funding, receiving a $4 million investment from Bridges Israel's impact fund.[89]

Impact is the Hallmark of this Generation

While not all these ventures yet measure their impact, they all incorporate it into their business models and the more of it they deliver, the more money they make. Many other such ventures across the world are showing incredible promise – from water to consumer goods, no sector is untouched by the ambition of young impact entrepreneurs.

Meena Sankaran, founder of the water quality monitoring start-up KETOS, was motivated to take action after contracting waterborne illnesses while growing up in India. With the creation of her company, which raised $9 million in 2019, she is working to use software and data analytics to flag water contamination at a fraction of the cost of other monitoring practices.[90] And water quality isn't just an issue in developing countries; dilapidated infrastructure in wealthier countries can also jeopardize water sources, as demonstrated by the water crisis in Flint, Michigan.[91] 'Smart water grid management ... is not just a nice-to-have; it's a must-have,' said Sankaran.[92]

The scale of impact that we can have on necessities such as water, air and food is enormous, but great impact can also be achieved in the field of consumer goods. TOMS shoes made the 'one-for-one' model famous – with every pair purchased, TOMS donates another pair to someone in need – and positive consumer reception helped the company's business model spread quickly. For example, after learning that socks were the most requested item at homeless shelters, American entrepreneurs Randy Goldberg and David Heath started Bombas in 2013, which sells high-end socks to consumers and also donates socks to homeless shelters – by 2019, they had donated over 20 million pairs.[93]

Another retail impact business model that has achieved traction is repurposing and selling items that would otherwise end up as landfill. In the UK, Elvis & Kresse is one such social enterprise that turns fire hoses, scrap leather and other second-hand materials into purses and wallets. Since 2005, the company has reimagined 175 tons of discarded fire hoses and has partnered with the fashion label Burberry to use their leather waste.[94] They also donate 50 per cent of their profits to charity.[95] 'When we set out to solve the fire-hose problem, we achieved that in five years. The leather problem is 80,000 times bigger,' said co-founder Kresse Wesling.[96] 'So not just my immediate future but my mid-range future is definitely going to be about solving this leather problem.'[97]

These impact business models will, in my view, become the hallmark of the millennial generation, which is following on the heels of brilliant young tech entrepreneurs such as Steve Jobs, Bill Gates, Larry Page and Mark Zuckerberg, who have driven high-tech to dizzying heights and changed all our lives in the process.

I can see great similarities between the disruption that high-tech brought to business and the disruption that impact is bringing today. I know we will see impact entrepreneurs that match the scale of the tech entrepreneurs' ambition and success, but surpass them in terms of the positive impact they have on the planet.

To date, the best-known impact entrepreneur is Elon Musk. For all his idiosyncrasies and the challenges Tesla, his high-end electric car company, has faced, Musk has single-handedly changed the automobile industry for the better.

According to Tesla's most recent impact report, the company has sold more than 550,000 electric vehicles, which have driven more than 10 billion miles between them. That translates to a saving of over four million metric tons of carbon dioxide compared with internal combustion engine vehicles.[98] Using the conventionally accepted cost to the environment of $300 per metric ton, this equates to $1.2 billion of avoided environmental damage.

The story of Musk and Tesla has inspired a new generation of entrepreneurs who are motivated to improve air quality and reduce our dependency on fossil fuels. From start-ups like Ather Energy in India – an electric bike scooter manufacturer that has been called 'The Tesla of two-wheelers'[99] – to more than a dozen Chinese car developers that are backed by billions of dollars in capital, the global stage is set for battery-powered travel to overpower the fuel-burning engine. 'Tesla paved the way,' said the head of one electric vehicle start-up based in Shanghai, 'and now we're taking this a step further.'[100]

Distinguishing Impact Businesses from Others

There has never been a better time to launch an impact business, in part because the legal and regulatory environment is becoming much friendlier, empowering businesses to go beyond their traditional legal obligation to seek profit alone. The most advanced effort is in the US, where B Lab has existed since 2006 'to serve those entrepreneurs who are using business as a force for good'. The 'B' stands for 'Beneficial'.

A global non-profit organization that grants private certification to for-profit companies that meet set standards for social and environmental performance, B Lab gives each business a score according to 180 different measures of impact. The scores reflect a company's ability to meet standards of social and environmental performance, accountability and transparency[101] – to be granted certification, they must receive a certain score, which is recertified every three years.

There are currently about 3,000 certified B Corps across 150 industries, in 64 countries – they include Patagonia, Warby Parker, Revolution Foods and Ben & Jerry's.[102]

As we will see in Chapter 4, even a big company like Danone has been able to obtain certification for three of its subsidiaries – its North American division is the biggest B Corp in the world. As a result of efforts by B Lab, a new corporate form was introduced in the US in 2010: the benefit corporation.

The benefit corporation's legal form frees businesses from the obligation to maximize profit, enabling them to seek impact at the same time, without having to fear legal action by shareholders.[103] Without the traditional mandate to maximize financial returns at all cost, benefit corporations are able to make decisions that reflect the interests of their workforce, community and the environment, in addition to being concerned with financial returns to shareholders. It provides legal protection for acting in accordance with their moral purpose.

In the United States, 34 states have already introduced benefit corporation legislation, and six more are in the process of doing so.[104] By the middle of 2019, more than 5,400 benefit corporations were active in America. Patagonia and Kickstarter are examples of companies that are both certified by B Lab and incorporated as benefit corporations.

A similar effort has taken place in the UK, with the introduction of Community Interest Companies (CIC) in 2005. The initiative is directed at small businesses and allows them to use their profits and assets for public good. In the first ten years after its launch, over 14,000 companies registered as CICs.[105] This trend of passing legislation to enhance the status of social enterprises is spreading to other countries, including France (which we will discuss in Chapter 6), Luxembourg and Italy.

Impact Entrepreneurial Networks

For any new business starting up, mentorship and seed investment are crucial. Recent decades have given rise to numerous kick-starter organizations that foster impact entrepreneurship in the early stages, as their groundbreaking innovations take shape. The non-profit Ashoka is a good example. Founded by Bill Drayton in 1980 with the aim of mitigating income inequality through social entrepreneurship, it identifies entrepreneurs who have large-scale solutions to social challenges, supporting them as they strive to achieve their vision. 'Ashoka Fellows' receive a financial stipend that allows them to devote themselves to implementing their social innovation, with the eventual aim of creating a self-sustaining institution.

Since its founding, Ashoka has built one of the largest global communities of social entrepreneurs, sponsoring over 3,500 in over 90 countries around the world.[106]

Echoing Green is another leader in the field. This global non-profit has since 1987 provided seed-stage funding and strategic support to organizations that have collectively served more than 12 million students in 3,700 schools, 3.7 million patients and 270,000 community health workers.[107] Notable Echoing Green fellows include Wendy Kopp, co-founder of Teach For America, a non-profit organization that trains college graduates and professionals to teach for two years in communities throughout the United States and beyond, in support of educational equity.

Another organization encouraging high-impact entrepreneurs is Endeavor. Founded by Linda Rottenberg in 1997, it spans 50 offices across the globe, identifying, mentoring and co-investing from its $115 million fund in the ventures of impact entrepreneurs.[108]

Together, pioneering organizations like Ashoka, Echoing Green and Endeavor have advanced the field of social impact entrepreneurship. These organizations have become role models for new efforts to drive impact entrepreneurship across the world and ingrain it in modern business thinking.

A Rising Generation of Impact Entrepreneurs

The state of our world demands that we embrace innovative solutions to society's most pressing challenges. For the young entrepreneur, the examples discussed in this chapter offer huge inspiration. Across the world, young entrepreneurs are bringing innovative solutions to our most vexing problems, capitalizing on the new technologies that their predecessors brought to the world. When entrepreneurs aim for profit and impact at the same time, they are able to define ways to succeed without sacrificing financial returns and are often turning their impact into a key driver of their success. Because they place impact at the core of their companies' business models, their profits grow together with their impact.

As the risk–return–impact model disrupts prevailing business thinking, and governments introduce new incentives to drive impact entrepreneurship, impact entrepreneurs will revolutionize our approaches to improving our world. The first generation of impact entrepreneurs is already showing how to accelerate social progress, make society fairer and reinforce the efforts of governments and philanthropists to improve lives and help the planet.

For those who are bold enough to lead the way, give yourself permission to try and fail, and above all to set ambitious goals of doing well *and* good at the same time. Your ventures will bring positive change, and you will also set an example in how to achieve a healthier balance between what we do for ourselves and what we do for others.

> Choose a problem that affects a large number of people and define a product or service that solves it

My motto is 'Start young, think big and stick with it'. Choose a problem that affects a large number of people and define a product or service that solves it. Put impact at the core of your business and measure it, rather than simply adding it as a parallel objective on which you keep an eye. Strive to achieve both deep and wide impact. That way, when your business succeeds, it will do so both because it is profitable and because of its impact. When the impact you create is intrinsic to your company's business, you can remain as focused as any other ambitious entrepreneur.

Impact will help you succeed. It will enable you to recruit the best talent, because talent is attracted to companies that also do good. The best start-ups are those that solve significant issues, because they are the most successful at attracting the most gifted teams and uniting them in pursuit of an inspiring mission. Finally, as impact investment gains momentum, investors will seek you out, because you are an early leader of an investment trend that will soon dominate financial markets.

There is one big difference between the past generation of young tech entrepreneurs and the rising generation of impact entrepreneurs: while tech entrepreneurs were able to thrive in only a few rarefied environments, such as Silicon Valley, impact entrepreneurs thrive wherever there are major social and environmental issues to tackle. They share the same passion and ambition to make a difference, and to lead an entrepreneurial movement that sets the norms for a new and better world.

Chapter 3

IMPACT INVESTING SETS THE NEW NORMAL

We must base our investment decisions on risk–return–impact

When BlackRock CEO Larry Fink, leader of the largest investment firm in the world, writes open letters urging businesses to consider their environmental impact, people take notice. When workers say they want to divert their pension savings away from harmful companies and toward socially responsible ones, pension funds pay attention. And when the world's biggest fossil fuel companies are pressured by a group of several hundred prominent investors to reduce their emissions, those companies are left with little choice but to comply.

What do these actions have in common? They were initiated by investors who felt a growing sense of responsibility for the world we share, and they mark a shift in how investors regard the companies in which they invest; they increasingly recognize that in order to change the world, they must also change the way they do business.

We can use the power of our individual positions to demand better from the businesses we support, and we can choose to channel capital into those that aim to make a positive impact on society and the planet – such as the ventures we explored in the preceding chapter. Instead of blaming the private sector, we can exercise our powerful collective sway to change it.

From the US to Japan, France, the UK, Scandinavia and the Netherlands, investors are starting to prioritize impact in their decision-making like never before. This positive and mounting energy is impressive – its scale is global and its pace is accelerating.

In recent years, institutional investors have significantly increased their commitment to Environmental Sustainable Governance (ESG) investing, also known as Responsible Investment (RI), whose main goal is to minimize harm. Investments are screened for negative impact in order to exclude bad actors, such as tobacco or coal companies or those that use child labor. Over the past two years, the ESG market has grown from \$22 trillion to \$31 trillion,[1] representing 15 per cent of all investable assets in the world and equivalent to more than a third of professionally managed assets.

Within ESG, growing investor demand for green bonds is an interesting indicator of the rise of this new way of investing. A green bond is a traditional bond that funds environmental projects. Investor demand for these bonds has skyrocketed, surpassing \$200 billion in 2019,[2] an increase of over 50 per cent over 2018[3] and reaching \$750 billion in total.

It is not surprising that Peter Harrison, the CEO of Schroders, a £450-billion ($598.5 billion) UK-based asset manager, recently declared that impact is now a 'megatrend' in the investment business.

But investors are, justifiably, concerned about 'impact washing', where existing activities are simply rebranded as impact, without there being any change in the impact that is delivered. So there is an urgent need to set the bar higher. We need to ensure that the intention to deliver impact translates into actual impact, and to be sure of achieving this, we must measure it. And this is where impact investing comes in.

Impact investing goes further than ESG investing in two ways: firstly, it aims not just to avoid a negative impact, but to create a positive one; secondly, it insists on measuring the impact it creates. ESG investments do not employ measurement but instead typically assess the effects of a company's policies in a qualitative and non-standardized way. Such assessment is inaccurate and it makes it impossible to rely on dependable comparisons between businesses. In contrast, true impact investment removes the guesswork and replaces it with dependable impact data. Since 2016, the impact investment market has doubled each year. In 2017, it was estimated at $230 billion; in 2018 it was $502 billion;[4] and now it is heading for the first $1 trillion.

The demand for impact investment is huge. The International Finance Corporation (IFC), a subsidiary of the World Bank, estimates that investor demand now amounts to no less than $26 trillion, 50 times the size of the 2018 market. With such a huge level of unmet demand, we can expect the market to continue to grow quickly for many more years.

The simple reason that some of the world's largest asset managers and pension funds are prioritizing impact is that their clients are demanding it, especially younger ones. According to a study by the US Trust, 'Millennials are investing in organizations that prioritize the greater good more than any previous generation,'[5] and a recent McKinsey report revealed that they are twice as likely to invest in companies that have a positive impact on society.[6] Millennials stand to inherit huge sums from their baby boomer parents over the next few decades: the sum is $30 trillion in the US alone.[7] As a result, millennials will be a major force in shifting the way their money is invested.

> Impact investment will become more than a moral choice – it will become a smart business decision

As impact investment managers show that they can deliver a desirable combination of impact and financial return, impact investment will become more than a moral choice – it will become a smart business decision. Investors will come to realize that we are able to increase returns not in spite of impact, but *because* of it.

How can this be? Well, as we discussed in the previous chapter, when we optimize risk–return–impact, we lower risk in a number of ways. Firstly, we avoid the risks that accompany investments that do harm: the risk of future regulation, taxation and even the prohibition of activities that could put a halt to business altogether. As just one example, one of the most sophisticated investors in the world, David Swensen from Yale University, recently wrote to the CEOs of Yale's portfolio companies to stress that climate change guides Yale's investment policy. He asked them to factor the impact of fossil fuels in their reporting – he is concerned that a carbon tax may be introduced, which would damage their profitability.

Another example of 'shareholder activism' towards polluting companies is the letter sent by Sir Christopher Hohn, one of the best-performing hedge fund managers in the world, to the CEOs of his portfolio companies. He demanded that they reduce their greenhouse gas emissions and disclose their carbon footprint. Investors, he says, 'can use their voting power to force change on companies who refuse to take their environmental emissions seriously. Investors have the power, and they have to use it.'[8] In short, doing harm has become risky business.

Irresponsible companies take another risk: the risk that consumers, employees and investors will leave them for competitors whose values are better aligned with their own. By choosing to prioritize impact, investors duck these risks too.

But impact can do more than reduce risk – it can also boost returns, by opening the door to new sets of opportunities. For example, a company that provides lower-cost products for underserved populations may not sound like a great investment opportunity, but, if it taps into a massive pool of latent demand, this may well allow it to grow more profitably than its competitors who serve more established markets.

As we saw in our discussion of impact ventures earlier, when we view the world through an impact lens, we discover opportunities to achieve higher growth and returns that we would otherwise pass by. In short, doing good can be excellent business.

From Measuring Risk to Measuring Impact

The measurement of risk, which began in the second half of the twentieth century,[9] had a profound effect on investment portfolios across the world. The new notion of risk-adjusted returns led investors to include higher-risk investment categories in their investment portfolios, when the expected return was sufficiently high. This thinking brought the idea of portfolio diversification, which in turn opened the door to new higher risk and return asset classes, including venture capital, private equity and investment in emerging countries. As a consequence of risk measurement, risk thinking brought higher levels of return than previously, when investment was limited to the stocks and bonds of one's own country, as had been the general practice until the 1970s.

This is relevant because impact can be measured even more dependably than risk and because, I believe, we are about to see it measured systematically in impact-weighted financial accounts, which will reflect a company's impact and its financial performance at the same time. Once such accounts start to take hold, impact thinking will have a momentous effect, just as risk thinking did previously: investment portfolios will change to deliver measurable social and environmental impact alongside financial returns.

The social impact bond, which we looked at in Chapter 1, is a good example of impact investment innovation. Since a SIB's return is based on the achievement of social or environmental outcomes, its returns are basically independent of movements in stock markets or interest rates. As a result,

SIBs reduce the volatility and improve the returns of a portfolio when the stock market takes a nosedive or interest rates soar.

Because of the importance of investment flows within our economies, risk–return–impact investing puts us on the road to impact economies

SIBs and DIBs also clearly demonstrate the inherent logic of risk–return–impact and that by optimizing this triple helix we can reach a higher 'efficient frontier', where for the same level of risk we can achieve higher returns and greater impact. Because of the importance of investment flows within our economies, risk–return–impact investing puts us on the road to impact economies, where impact influences every decision taken in investment and as a consequence, as we will see in the next chapter, in business too.

Raising the Bar

Several forces are already at work to raise the impact bar, and the World Bank is chief among them. Under the inspired leadership of Kristalina Georgieva, the World Bank's IFC launched its substantive report 'The Promise of Impact', together with its 'Operating Principles for Impact Management', in April 2019.

The latter is designed to provide 'a market standard for impact investing'. It emphasizes the importance of independent verification of outcomes achieved and aims for 'investors [to] seek to generate positive impact for society alongside financial returns in a disciplined and transparent way'.[10] These three words, 'verification', 'disciplined' and 'transparent', are essential to driving higher standards in impact investment.

To date, the IFC's Operating Principles have been adopted by more than 80 global investors[11] – including multilateral development institutions, banks, corporations, insurance companies and asset managers. Collectively, these organizations hold over $350 billion of impact investments, a figure which is equal to 70 per cent of the global total.[12] The IFC's CEO, Philippe Le Houérou, has declared, 'there is now potential to bring impact investing into the mainstream.'

Focus on the SDGs

In 2015, the impact investing movement gained focus and urgency with the release of the United Nations Sustainable Development Goals (SDGs) to improve our world. Leaders around the globe came together to set the agenda for building a more just and sustainable future. By 2030, these goals aim to hit a number of targets across 17 areas, including zero poverty and hunger, water and energy for all, inclusive and equitable quality education, environmental stewardship and protection of human rights.

It has been estimated that financing the achievement of the SDGs will require an additional $30 trillion in investment over the next decade. The huge financial resources of the private sector are necessary to reach this number – this money cannot come from government and philanthropy alone. If we can get the $31 trillion of ESG investment to deliver real impact, the private sector can fill that gap. To do so, we need to bring impact measurement to ESG investment flows.

To put the $30 trillion into perspective, the global investment pool is estimated at $215 trillion. As we have already mentioned, philanthropic foundations give away around $150 billion globally each year,[13] while OECD governments spend $10 trillion a year on health and education alone.

2016 – Sources of Investment Capital* (USD trillion)

Pension funds	38.3
Insurance companies	29.4
Sovereign wealth funds	7.4
High-net-worth individuals	72.3
Mass affluent	67.2
Total assets	**214.6**
of which:	
Global assets under management	**85**

*Asset and Wealth Management Revolution: Embracing Exponential Change, PWC report (2017)

2018 – Size of Financial Markets (USD trillion)

Global value of quoted shares*	74.7
Bond Market	102.8
Private Investments** – Venture Capital & Private Equity – Real Estate – Infrastructure	5
Total	**182.5**

*SIMFA – Capital Markets Fact Book (2019)
**McKinsey Global Private Markets Review (2018)

As rigorous impact measurement advances within the current ESG pool, converting it into impact investment, and new forms of impact investment develop beyond it, impact investment should be able to exceed 20 per cent of the world's investment assets during the 2020s, taking us to more than $40 trillion. But how exactly will we get there?

Whether we are a worker with a pension, invest money through an asset manager, have a life insurance policy or are wealthy enough to invest through our own family office, we all have an influence on our investment portfolios. By exercising this influence to avoid companies that do harm and seek out companies that do good, we can help finance the achievement of the SDGs and contribute directly to a more equitable and sustainable world.

So far, the investor groups that demonstrate the greatest progress towards impact investing are pension funds ($38.3 trillion) and asset managers ($85 trillion). Let's start with pension funds.

Pension Funds

When we hear the words 'pension fund', what comes to mind? Most of us are completely unaware of how our pensions are invested and of the impact our pension fund portfolio is having on the world, yet the actions of our pension fund managers have an outsized impact. The world's pension funds held $38 trillion in 2016,[14] nearly 20 per cent of the world's total investment assets. If our pension fund managers were to optimize risk–return–impact, they could significantly support the achievement of the SDGs – and there is no reason why we should not exercise more influence over how the money in our pensions is being invested.

In fact, a significant portion of those of us with pensions want their managers to align with their values. A 2017 report by Big Society Capital in the UK found that almost half of all savers want to invest in companies that reflect their values, with health, social care, environmental projects and housing the preferred areas.[15] Some of us are turning this desire into action, which is reflected in the changing approaches of pension fund managers across the world. Under this pressure and in light of the trend for ESG investment, they are beginning to change the shape of their investment portfolios.

European pension fund managers, and Dutch ones in particular, are leading the way in this regard. When the UN announced the SDGs in 2015, the Dutch created a plan of action to advance the goals: a group of pension funds, insurance companies and banks got together and launched the Dutch SDG Investing Agenda in December 2016.

The agenda is groundbreaking in its creation of a national consensus to support sustainable investment. It boasts 18 signatories, who together manage more than $3 trillion of assets, including some of the leading pension funds in the Netherlands: PGGM, which manages €218 billion ($242 billion),[16] APG, which manages €505 billion ($561 billion),[17] and MN, which manages €130 billion ($144 billion).

On signing the SDG Investing Agenda, Gerald Cartigny, the chief investment officer of MN, expressed the thinking behind it: 'Focusing on financial return alone is not enough to guarantee quality of life for future pensioners. We are intrinsically motivated to integrate sustainability in our investment portfolios and contribute to SDGs where possible.'[18]

PGGM, one of the world's leading impact-driven pension funds, has invested approximately €12 billion ($13.3 billion),[19] in line with the four SDG themes of climate, food security, water scarcity, and health, and has a mandate to invest at least €20 billion ($22.2 billion) in total.[20] Piet Klop, senior advisor for responsible investment, says the organization is undergoing a shift in culture and that 'it's quite something to hold ourselves accountable and pursue measurement and eventually management of impact.'[21]

In a similar way, PME, another Dutch pension fund that represents the metal and electrical engineering industry, announced in early 2017 that it would align 10 per cent of its €45 billion ($50 billion) portfolio with the SDGs. This new strategy will focus on affordable and sustainable energy, work and economic growth, sustainable innovation and sustainable cities. By the end of 2018, PME reported that 8.8 per cent of its investments were contributing to the SDGs, and that it aims to hit 10 per cent soon.[22]

The Dutch civil service pension fund, ABP, has stated that it wants to double the assets allocated to 'high-sustainability investments', to €58 billion ($64 billion). Its priorities include reducing its carbon footprint, investing in education, promoting safe working conditions, respecting human rights and eradicating child labor.[23] ABP also announced that it will divest its entire holdings in tobacco and nuclear weapons – worth an estimated €3.3 billion ($3.7 billion) – and several other large Dutch funds have also cut tobacco firms from their portfolios in recent years.[24]

An increasing number of pension funds in other countries, including Norway's KLP, Sweden's AP funds, Denmark's Pension Danmark and the National Employment Savings Trust (NEST) in the UK, are also heading in the same direction, emphasizing the particular concerns of their pension savers. So it is that NEST has started to shift its assets into a 'climate aware' investment strategy that invests less in companies that are responsible for high carbon emissions, and more in renewable energy companies.[25] Mark Fawcett, the fund's chief investment officer, has pointed out that NEST's youngest investors are just 17 years old and suggests that 'as responsible long-term investors on behalf of our members, we can't afford to ignore climate change risks and we've committed to being part of the solution.'

In the UK, the pension fund of HSBC bank has made a climate-tilted fund the usual option for its younger investors.[26] About 60 per cent of them are under 40, so the fund believes that its focus on climate will appeal to them and make them more engaged with their investment choices.[27]

As Mark Thompson, the fund's chief investment officer at the time, said, 'one of our board's investment beliefs is that incorporating the management of ESG risk into our standard investment process is consistent with our fiduciary duty.'

Because of how most pension funds are designed, employers end up having an enormous amount of influence over their employees' investing choices. They typically choose the financial institution they are going to work with, which narrows down the employees' choices considerably. Furthermore, as many as 60 per cent of retirement savers in countries like the US are enrolled in savings plans automatically;[28] for these investors, the employers have made all the choices about where they put their money. And most of them do not choose socially responsible investment options, let alone impact investments.

To redress this situation, the French have come up with a new model that makes impact investing accessible to pension savers. The 90/10 'solidarity funds' allocate 10 per cent of their assets to organizations with a special 'solidarity label' similar to impact investments, and invests the remaining 90 per cent in traditional companies that meet socially responsible investing guidelines. Companies with more than 50 employees must offer a 90/10 fund as an option for members.[29] By 2018, over one million people had invested in these funds, investment in which totaled nearly €10 billion ($ 11.1 billion).[30]

This approach could easily be replicated across the world. Its attraction is that it enables pension contributors to have 90 per cent of their assets in ESG investing, while dipping their toe in impact investing at the same time. For this reason, Big Society Capital (BSC) and other investors in the UK are advocating 'social pension funds' that follow the French 'solidarity' model.[31]

Though the US is lagging behind Europe, some of the biggest and most influential American pension funds are moving in a similar direction. The California Public Employees' Retirement System (CalPERS) represents more than 1.9 million members[32] and manages more than $380 billion.[33] It is one of the biggest pension funds in the US, so when it takes action, the market notices.[34] The fund uses its power and influence as a major shareholder to push corporations to change their behavior and do the right thing.

For example, CalPERS is a key player in Climate Action 100+, a group of institutional investors that is trying to encourage fossil fuel companies to change their policies.[35] So far, the group has won commitments from several major companies: Royal Dutch Shell has committed to specific targets for lowering its emissions; the mining company Glencore has agreed to stop expanding its coal business; and Maersk, a shipping container company, has committed to carbon neutrality by 2050.

CalPERS 'sister fund', the California State Teachers' Retirement System (CalSTRS), manages $283 billion[36] and it too has taken on the ESG mantle. It explicitly takes a list of

21 ESG factors into account when evaluating the risk of an investment.[37] For example, CalSTRS considers it a risk to the long-term returns of an investment if a company discriminates based on race, gender, disability or other factors, or pays 'inadequate attention to the impacts of climate change'.

Like CalPERS, CalSTRS has used its influence to push companies to take action. Along with the Jana Partners hedge fund, CalSTRS wrote a letter to the board of directors of Apple, asking the company to do more to ensure that children are using its products safely.[38] Citing research that has associated the use of iPhones with an inability to pay attention in class, as well as more serious health risks including depression and even suicide, the investors wrote, 'We believe there is a clear need for Apple to offer parents more choices and tools to help them ensure that young consumers are using your products in an optimal manner.' The letter brought worldwide attention to these issues and put significant pressure on Apple to act, given that the two funds owned $2 billion in Apple stock between them.

CalSTRS' policies require it to try to engage with companies before selling shares, but divestment is always an option. As CalSTRS board member and California state treasurer John Chiang says, 'Engagement is an important and crucial first step, but these conversations must result in real action, otherwise divestment and other actionable options must be kept on the table.'

Of course, as the chief investment officer of CalSTRS Christopher Ailman notes, making change this way is 'darn hard and it's slow', so CalSTRS is moving to make an increasing number of investments that are impact-driven. In 2017 it bought its first social bond, issued by an arm of the World

Bank, which will invest in companies that source products from smallholder farms and provide affordable health and education services to low-income populations. 'Using financial vehicles that provide the potential for us to do well, while also doing good, is a double win for us,' says Ailman.

But the star of the scene in many ways is Japan's Government Pension Investment Fund (GPIF), the world's largest pension fund, with $1.5 trillion under management.[39] The fund's chief investment officer, Hiro Mizuno, is a great believer in the teachings of Ninomiya Sontoku, the nineteenth-century Japanese philosopher who held that 'economics without ethics is a crime, and ethics without economics is a fantasy.'[40]

Mizuno is one of impact's greatest champions in the world of pension funds. In 2017, GPIF raised its allocation to environmentally and socially responsible investments from 3 to 10 per cent of its stock holdings, an increase from 1 trillion yen ($9.5 billion) to 3.5 trillion yen ($33.3 billion). This was a big boost for ESG investing globally, as well as a potential generator of future ESG investments if smaller Asian pension funds follow suit.[41]

Through its ESG investment strategy, GPIF has selected various indexes including the FTSE Blossom Japan Index, constructed using international ESG standards such as the UN Sustainable Development Goals;[42] the MSCI Japan Empowering Women Index (WIN); and the MSCI Japan ESG Select Leaders Index, which targets companies with the best ESG profile in their sector.[43]

While these examples show that some in the conservative pension fund world have begun to be attracted to the new thinking about risk–return–impact, they are very much in the minority. Because pension fund trustees are accountable to their savers, as savers we have the power to exercise direct influence on how our portfolios are invested – and now is the time to use that power.

Asset Management Firms Take Impact to the Mainstream

When we talk about shifting investment to risk–return–impact, pension funds are one of the two big players in the room today; the other is asset managers. Investing for impact is becoming increasingly mainstream among big-name asset management firms. UBS, currently the world's largest private wealth manager[44] with $2.7 trillion in assets,[45] has stated publicly that sustainability is a 'cornerstone' of its business[46] and has set a goal of raising $5 billion in impact investing to advance the SDGs. It has already raised $325 million for the Rise Fund, the TPG-managed impact investment fund co-founded by Bono, lead singer of U2 and an outstandingly active philanthropist, who has become a powerful advocate for the use of impact investment to achieve social progress.

UBS has been a champion of the SDGs and strongly believes that private capital is critical in meeting these goals. As of 2018, UBS's ESG assets had tripled, from $63 billion to over $200 billion.[47] 'More and more, ESG is becoming integral to driving our client engagements,' says Michael Baldinger, the company's head of sustainable and impact investing.

Because a lack of information can prevent private inves-tors from taking the plunge into impact investing,[48] UBS helped create Align17, a digital marketplace for impact investment opportunities.[49] Its Optimus Foundation was also the investor in the Educate Girls Development Impact Bond, which has supported education in India (as we will discuss in Chapter 5). Following on the success of that bond, UBS invested in two other Indian DIBs, one designed to reduce infant and maternal mortality in Rajasthan[50] and the other to improve education.[51]

Goldman Sachs is another big-name asset management firm that is involved in impact investing. It was a lead investor in the first SIB in the US, which was aimed at reducing recid-ivism among released inmates of Rikers Island, New York City's main jail complex.[52] In 2016, Goldman Sachs acquired the impact investment advisory firm Imprint Capital.[53] At that time, they had about $500 million in ESG assets; by 2017, that number had skyrocketed to $10.6 billion.[54] According to John Goldstein, the co-founder of Imprint Capital, big inves-tors are increasingly looking to put more of their assets into socially responsible investing. 'Instead of saying "Why can't we do this with a small portion of our assets?", they asked, "Why can't we do this with our whole portfolio?"' Goldstein says. In a similar move, Schroders, the UK-based asset manager, has recently purchased Blue Orchard Finance, a specialist in microfinance.

The growing interest in impact investing is also evident in specialist corners of the market. Big-name private equity firms are moving into impact. Some are launching special-ized impact funds; among them are TPG, which has raised approximately $4 billion so far, Bain Capital, KKR and Partners Group. Going further, Megan Starr, the global head of impact for the Carlyle Group, announced that 'it's no longer possible to generate high rates of return unless you invest for impact. It reflects the economic reality'.[55] These firms' impact funds are being supported by big institutional investors, as well as high-net-worth individuals and their family offices. According to the 2017 Global Family Office Report, 40 per cent of family offices were planning to increase their allocation to impact investing in the next year.[56]

Sara Ferrari, head of the global family office group at UBS, has said that this shift reflects the increasing influence of millennials over their families' affairs. 'This is an opportunity for family offices to use their investment expertise to convert social objectives into financial concepts,' Ferrari said. 'In doing so, they can help to shape the purpose of a family and promote unity.' With the world's billionaires set to hand down $3.4 trillion, 40 per cent of total billionaire wealth, to their heirs over the next 20 years, this trend will only continue to gather momentum.

Big-name firms are taking action to make ESG and sustainable investing accessible to ordinary investors too: Bank of America, Merrill Lynch and Morgan Stanley are both offering ESG funds with various impact themes to their smaller clients. As an example, Morgan Stanley has launched an Investing with Impact Platform, offering over 120 investment products that are aligned with a variety of values-based themes, from 'Catholic Values' and gender equality to climate-change-aware investing.[57] The company has also developed an online education course for financial advisors, which has been designed to help them learn more about ESG invest-ing.[58] Educating financial advisors would help to democratize impact investing, since millions of Americans rely on them in managing their money.

The biggest of all the asset management firms, BlackRock, which has nearly $7 trillion under management, is confident that impact investing is the future. 'Sustainable investing will be a core component for how everyone invests in the future,' CEO Larry Fink has said.[59] Fink believes that sustainable investing, another name for ESG, does not mean sacrificing returns. 'We are going to see evidence over the long term that sustainable investing is going to be at least equivalent to core investments. I believe personally it will be higher,' he has said.

A growing number of new specialist impact investing firms are helping to demonstrate how impact investment can deliver market rates of return. Since their emergence in the early 2000s, these firms have helped to pave the way for today's large-scale asset managers, their track records giving credibility to the field. Some of their leaders came from the world of investment, while others came from the world of social entrepreneurship. Together they exemplify different investment approaches in how to deliver both impact and financial returns.

A notable leader of this group is Generation Investment Management, a sustainable investment management firm founded by Al Gore and David Blood in 2004, which manages about $20 billion. It promotes a vision of 'Sustainable Capitalism' – 'a financial and economic system within which businesses and investors seek to maximize long-term value creation, accounting for all material ESG metrics.'[60]

Another specialist global impact investor, Triodos Investment Management (€3.5 billion ($3.9 billion) assets under management),[61] is a subsidiary of the Dutch environmental Triodos Bank, which was founded in 1980.[62] Their strategy includes supporting green and renewable energy, promoting inclusive finance by providing credit to micro-entrepreneurs[63] and backing green and sustainable farming practices.[64]

Bridges Fund Management,[65] which I co-founded, is another early leader in the impact investment arena. Since 2002, it has used impact investment as a tool to address big societal challenges, raising more than £1 billion[66] ($1.33 billion) to invest in small and medium-sized enterprises, real estate and social sector organizations in the UK, USA and Israel,[67] creating jobs in underserved areas, delivering better health and education outcomes and finding innovative ways to reduce carbon emissions – all while still delivering a strong commercial performance.[68]

There are other specialist impact investment pioneers. LeapFrog Investments, founded in 2007 by Andy Kuper, invests in financial tools and healthcare services to underserved consumers in Asia and Africa and has put together a portfolio that currently reaches over 180 million people.[69] The California-based DBL Partners, which was founded in 2004 and is led by Nancy Pfund, has, as the acronym suggests, a 'double bottom line' investment strategy: it targets top-tier venture capital returns as well as positive social, environmental and economic impact, and counts Tesla as one of its investees.[70]

Social Capital, another West Coast venture capital firm, founded in 2011 by the former Facebook executive Chamath Palihapitiya, invests in innovative technology enterprises that are tackling some of 'the world's hardest problems'.[71] Acumen, a New York-based non-profit venture firm founded by Jacqueline Novogratz in 2001, addresses the problems of global poverty, agriculture, education, energy, healthcare, housing, water and sanitation in Asia, Africa and Latin America. Further names to note are Root Capital, which was founded in 1999 in Massachusetts and focuses on rural farmers, and Avishkaar, which was founded in 2001 and focuses on development in India's underserved regions.[72]

These specialist impact firms are the frontrunners of the movement. They demonstrate the logic, power and success of impact investing, and spur bigger firms to move beyond our outdated risk–return model to adopt one of risk–return–impact.

Resetting Investment for a New Reality

As we can see, investment leaders are moving in the direction of impact. Asset managers are introducing products that respond to their clients' desire for investments that improve lives and the planet, while also delivering attractive financial returns. The arrival of impact-weighted accounts, which we will explore in detail in the next chapter, will provide accurate data for their investment decisions and enable them to direct their investment to companies that deliver positive impact.

The concept of risk–return–impact is rapidly becoming the new normal for mainstream investors. To change the world, we must first change how we do business – starting with where and how we invest our money. Many are rallying around the SDGs. Investors around the world are adopting these goals as their own, reshaping their investment strategies and product offerings. And as institutional investors adopt impact in their investment strategies, they drive huge change in the global economy, turning impact economies into a fast-approaching reality.

> To change the world, we must first change how we do business – starting with where and how we invest our money

Just as the changing values of consumers prompted investors to shift their investment from companies with negative impacts to those with positive ones, the actions of investors are, in their turn, influencing the companies in which they invest to embed impact in their businesses. This is the next stop on our journey through the Impact Revolution.

Chapter 4

EMBEDDING IMPACT IN BUSINESS

Impact can be measured and compared

'A revolution is cooking – what are we going to do about it?' Emmanuel Faber, the CEO of Danone, issued this rallying cry at the Consumer Goods Forum in Berlin in 2017.[1] The leader of the French food multinational argued that while the food industry can be proud of some achievements – such as increased access to nutrition – it also bears much of the responsibility for the spread of diabetes and obesity, and the depletion of our planet's resources.[2]

'Food is precious,' Faber said, 'and we called it a commodity. We made it a consumer good. We let market forces drive demand and drive supply. And we are hard-wired for salt, for fat, for sugar... The system has reached its limits and we are pushing through these limits, so why don't we stop? We don't because the consumer doesn't realize. The consumer does not realize because the food system has disconnected people from their food.'[3]

Not content to call out the food industry for pushing unhealthy, commoditized products, he also argued for a complete redefinition of the purpose of business. 'The ultimate goal of the market economy cannot be anything other than social justice,' he said. 'This is a matter of business sense.'[4]

Faber wasn't just scolding his competitors. He admitted that though Danone's company signature was 'One Planet. One Health', 'You could say, "Nice intent. Where's the proof?" And you would be right.' As he also confessed, 'I'm ashamed at many of the decisions I continue to make. We are so far from being perfect.'[5]

By the time Faber gave this impassioned speech, Danone, which has four business lines (Essential Dairy and Plant-Based Products, Early Life Nutrition, Waters and Medical Nutrition) and generated $28 billion in revenue in 2017, had already begun experimenting with social impact projects – albeit on a small scale.[6]

Two years later, in August 2019, an influential group of 181 CEOs of some of America's largest companies known as the Business Roundtable, chaired by the JP Morgan CEO Jamie Dimon, issued a statement on the purpose of the corporation.[7] Between them, these companies employ more than 15 million people and make more than $7 trillion each year.[8] The Business Roundtable is a powerful and conservative representative of big business that since 1997 has reinforced the idea that 'corporations exist principally to serve shareholders' – in other words, that business exists to make money.

The 2019 statement upended that principle, suggesting that businesses have responsibilities not just to shareholders but to customers, employees, suppliers and communities. 'Each of our stakeholders is essential,' the statement read. 'We commit to deliver value to all of them, for the future success of our companies, our communities and our country.'

In the same week as the Business Roundtable statement was released, the French president Emmanuel Macron convened a meeting, which I attended, of 34 companies at the Elysée Palace to launch an initiative called Business for Inclusive Growth. This group of big hitters employ more than three million people, with revenues of more than $1 trillion. They came together to fight against inequality by 'advancing human rights in direct employment and supply chains; building inclusive workplaces; and strengthening inclusion in company value chains and business ecosystems',[9] and have since pledged to take real steps in support of economic equality and social inclusion.[10]

There is hardly a company boardroom in the world where the subject of impact is not being actively discussed

These initiatives follow efforts 'to create new norms of corporate leadership' by the B Team, an organization founded in 2012 by prominent business leaders like Paul Polman and Richard Branson.

What is making all these CEOs change their priorities and focus on the impact their businesses have on their employees, their communities and the environment rather than simply on profit? In short, they can see that the values of consumers and employees have changed, and also that this has not been lost on investors. They are now beginning to realize that they must deliver positive impact if they want to survive.

As we've already seen, investors are directing $31 trillion to companies that seek to create positive impact. And when investors talk, businesses listen. There is hardly a company boardroom in the world where the subject of impact is not being actively discussed.

The massive shift in consumer behavior is clear for all to see. A recent study by Unilever found that a third of consumers buy products by brands that they believe are doing social or environmental good.[11] Many other surveys have identified the same trend: consumers increasingly want to support companies that treat their workers well and have a positive impact on society and the planet.

Today, it's easier for consumers to align their purchases with their values than ever before – there are even apps to help you. For example, Buycott – an app that lets you 'vote with your wallet'[12] that was launched by the 27-year-old programmer Ivan Pardo in 2013, allows you to scan any barcode and access information about the company that produces the product. Does the company treat its workers properly? Does it test its products on animals? Does it support human rights causes? And so on.[13] Buycott allows users to 'shop with their conscience' across 192 countries, crowdsourcing product information from consumers.[14]

As Pardo puts it, 'Every dollar you spend is a vote for the type of world you want to see. I think that if you're spending dollars buying products that support things that are against your values then you're complicit in allowing those values to be the norm ... What we hope to accomplish is to allow people to leverage their purchase decisions to create change in the world.'[15]

A recent Accenture report on the rise of purpose-led brands calls this the 'era of radical visibility', and states that 'companies are under the spotlight like never before as they struggle for competitive advantage in the context of this reality'.[16]

This radical visibility has created a wave of change across a wide variety of consumer products. Coca-Cola is reducing the sugar content of its drinks.[17] Nestlé is reducing the salt and sugar levels in its products.[18] Mars is launching healthier snacks,[19] while acquiring a minority stake in the healthy snack-bar company Kind.[20] Nike is using recycled materials in its apparel and Lego is developing 'sustainable bricks' that are made from plant-based plastic.

Unilever, under the enlightened leadership of CEO Paul Polman, has overhauled whole product lines to reduce their negative impact on the environment. In 2013, the company launched 'compressed deodorants' for their Sure, Dove and Vaseline brands[21] that use 50 per cent less gas and 25 per cent less packaging, cutting each can's carbon footprint by approximately 25 per cent. What's more, the company has invited other manufacturers to use compressed technology in their own aerosols, providing a 'how-to guide' to help others adopt the technology and even sharing the details about which suppliers helped bring their product to market.[22]

As well as reducing its own environmental footprint, Unilever is also helping its consumers do the same through water-saving products. In developing and emerging countries where water is scarce, around 40 per cent of domestic water is used to wash clothes by hand, and rinsing to remove soap suds accounts for about 70 per cent of that water use. Enter SmartFoam, a new anti-foam molecule that breaks down soap suds more quickly, enabling families to use less water every day.

Other multinational businesses are developing new sustainable packaging materials. In 2017, Nestlé Waters started working with Danone and a start-up called Origin Materials in a research consortium called the NaturALL Bottle Alliance, which was formed to develop a bio-based plastic bottle made from 100 per cent renewable materials. With the technology already proven at a pilot level, they are well on their way to commercial-scale production.[23]

At the same time, other multinationals including Coca-Cola are working to produce 100 per cent plant-based plastics at commercial scale. Coca-Cola has been producing a partially bio-based bottle since 2009: the PlantBottle is a fully recyclable bottle that is composed of 30 per cent plant materials.[24] Between 2009 and 2015, more than 35 billion of them were distributed in nearly 40 countries, avoiding more than 315,000 metric tons of carbon dioxide emissions.[25] The market for bio-based plastic is projected to reach $13 billion by 2023.[26]

Given the growing consumer interest in such positive-impact products, it is no surprise that integrating impact is good for business. Unilever's 'Sustainable Living' brands, which include Knorr, Dove and Lipton, are growing 50 per cent faster than their other brands and delivering more than 60 per cent of the company's growth.[27] Far from limiting their options, their effort to view their product lines through an impact lens actually opens the door to new opportunities that can boost their growth and profitability.

The benefits of impact thinking go beyond the bottom line; embedding impact into a business can reduce the long-term risk from new regulation and taxation that might, for example, penalize the use of plastics. It can also lead to increased productivity, cost savings from waste reduction, greater efficiency in the supply chain, and improved talent acquisition and retention.

It should come as no surprise then that companies with B Corp certification are often better able to attract talented employees.[28] Millennials make up half of the American workforce.[29] According to the 2016 Cone Communications Millennial Employee Engagement Study, 75 per cent of them say they would take a pay cut to work for a responsible company, versus 55 per cent of non-millennials.[30]

But what does becoming a responsible business actually mean? What distinguishes a company that is responsible to multiple stakeholders from a shareholder-focused company that donates money to a few charitable causes? And how does an impact-oriented business differ from a traditional one that engages in philanthropy through its corporate social responsibility (CSR) budget?

Michael Porter, professor of strategy at Harvard Business School and a leading thinker on the role of impact in business, lays out a clear vision of what he calls 'shared value':[31] 'While philanthropy and CSR focus efforts on "giving back" or minimizing the harm business has on society, shared value focuses company leaders on maximizing the competitive value of solving social problems,' whether that be through 'new customers and markets, cost savings, talent retention, and more'.[32]

Businesses that take CSR seriously generally do so to demonstrate corporate citizenship – they are giving away a portion of their profits rather than fundamentally changing the way they do business. Businesses that are seeking to integrate impact generally start by examining their products and services or the environmental effects of their operations. The most advanced are moving to embed impact throughout their whole business, setting measurable impact targets against defined benchmarks to move their businesses away from generating negative impact and focusing on increasing their positive impact.

Many of these companies are finding new opportunities to solve social problems by developing business models that have impact at their core. In Michael Porter's words, 'The purpose of the corporation must be redefined as creating shared value, not just profit per se. This will drive the next wave of innovation and productivity growth in the global economy.'[33]

The most innovative business leaders are proving that their companies can increase their impact and their profit at the same time. However, since the shift from risk–return to risk–return–impact affects every aspect of a business including its products and operations, those businesses that are beginning to move in the direction of impact are doing so in different ways and starting in different areas.

Let us take a closer look at some of these businesses: Danone and IKEA endeavor to integrate impact across their entire company, while Chobani and Adidas strive to deliver impact through a specific aspect of their business.

Facing Reality

In 2005, Emmanuel Faber, then Asia-Pacific president of Danone, arranged a lunch between the company's CEO Franck Riboud and the Nobel laureate Muhammad Yunus, known around the world as the father of microfinance.[34] At the meal, Yunus invited Riboud 'to come to Bangladesh and build his first social business enterprise'.[35] Riboud agreed, and in 2006, Grameen and Danone announced the creation of Grameen Danone Foods Social Business Enterprise.[36]

Bangladesh has one of the world's highest rates of malnutrition; to combat this problem, the venture aimed to provide children with affordable and nutritious cups of yoghurt,[37] with Danone committing to reinvest any profit into other like-minded initiatives.[38]

For a major multinational, the venture was tiny – the yoghurt factory in Bogra was 1 per cent of the size of a typical Danone plant, and its production capacity was limited.[39] But the project punched above its weight in terms of innovation – the plant's designer, a long-time Danone executive, said it was 'more advanced than the huge plants I have designed in Brazil, Indonesia, China and India'.[40]

The product itself was innovative, too. Danone had to figure out how to pack vitamin A, iron, zinc and iodine into the yoghurt without making it sour, keep it refrigerated during shipping and find ways to produce it as cheaply as possible, in order to keep consumer prices below 10 cents.[41]

A decade after its opening, the enterprise was selling 100,000 cups of yoghurt every day, buying milk from nearly 500 local farmers and employing 250 women to sell the product door-to-door.[42] And drinking one cup of the fortified yoghurt per day was helping the children of Bogra grow taller.[43]

As one journalist reported, the 'tiny factory' was 'giving the company a profitable lesson in manufacturing for the developing world – and even some tips for business in the West', in areas such as factory design and product development.[44]

To invest in Grameen Danone and similar social enterprises, Danone created a group of mutual funds to support social innovation under its Danone Communities entity. In collaboration with Crédit Agricole, one of the largest French banks, the fund launched with €50 million ($55.5 million) – €30 million from institutional investors and €20 million from Danone – and focused on investing in socially responsible businesses. By 2018, Danone Communities had supported 11 businesses in 15 countries,[45] 'to alleviate malnutrition, make drinking water safe and break the cycle of poverty where we operate'.[46]

In 2008, the company established the Danone Fund for Nature, a €40 million ($44.4 million) fund created with conservation organizations, with the ambition to 'restore degraded ecosystems, redevelop local economies and combat climate change'.[47] Then, in 2015, Danone and Mars Inc. created the Livelihoods Fund for Family Farming, in order to help improve the livelihoods of smallholder farmers in their supply chain.[48] The €120 million ($133.2 million) evergreen fund was opened to companies, impact investors and public development institutions.[49]

Faber believes that Danone's work in social impact has made the company stronger in talent retention because

Danone employees identify with the impact mission, in creating innovations that can be implemented companywide, in breathing new energy into the company and in gaining fresh perspectives from people who question processes and ultimately improve them.[50]

For social impact to work at the level of global enterprise, Faber believes it is necessary 'to have the very broad vision that you're not doing this for CSR, communication, PR... or even your good conscience as a person'.[51] The real reason to pursue social impact at the global enterprise level, Faber believes, is if a company's leaders come to realize that they are divorced from reality.[52] As he says, 'Our planet's resources are not infinite, mistreated employees and suppliers will not be the most productive, and operating an enterprise without the well-being of its consumers in mind is a deeply flawed business plan.'

This line of thinking has pushed Danone to pursue impact across its main operations. In 2018, its North American operations joined Danone's British and Spanish subsidiaries as a B Corp, and it is now the largest one in the world. The parent company now has its sights set on becoming the first multinational B Corp.[53]

Danone is among Forbes's largest 250 corporations in the world and is rated as having the third-highest impact on public health and nutrition,[54] so its aim to bring 'health through food'[55] is having significant effect. It demonstrated its emphasis on providing nutritious food products through its $12.5 billion acquisition of organic food producer WhiteWave in 2017, the company's largest purchase in a decade.[56] The acquisition makes Danone the world's biggest producer of organic food[57] and puts it in a good position to satisfy growing consumer demand for a plant-based and dairy-free lifestyle, motivated by environmental, ethical and health concerns.[58]

Faber's mission to improve the impact Danone has on the world, includes not just human but also ecological health. In presenting a new policy regarding its packaging in 2016, Faber said, 'Our ambition is to create a second life for all the plastic packaging we put on the market, so that we move toward 100 per cent recycling in this respect. Part of the plan is also to launch a 100 per cent bio-sourced second-generation plastic.'[59]

All such impact transitions require the setting of clear, measurable goals. Danone has announced that it is linking its impact goals to the SDGs:[60] it has committed to be carbon neutral by 2050 and has set intermediate targets for 2030, building on a 50 per cent reduction in emissions from its operations, packaging and logistics between 2008 and 2016.[61] Faber has said in an interview that setting ambitious goals with long-term horizons has been essential to the company's progress: 'We would never have made as much progress with our carbon dioxide reduction program in 2008 if we had just gone for a 2 per cent reduction per year rather than 30 per cent over five years, which we set ourselves.'[62]

At a conference in 2014, the year that he became CEO, Faber summarized his philosophy: 'The economy without the social side is barbarism; the social side without the economy is utopia.'[63] As Faber himself put it in his speech at the Consumer Goods Forum in Berlin, 'Unlike what Wall Street is trying to tell us, there is no invisible hand. In particular, there is no invisible hand when it comes to [doing] the right or the wrong thing.'[64]

A much younger American yoghurt company, Chobani, is approaching the creation of positive impact by starting to deliver it through its employment.

Accountability, Community, Gratitude

At the end of 2012, two refugee sisters arrived in the US from the Middle East, seeking a new life.[65] Nisa and Amna's long and arduous journey began with threats of acid attacks and death and included being stowed in the windowless compartment of a truck without air enough to breathe – in fact, one child packed in tight with them died in transit.[66]

Smugglers had separated the girls from their mother during their journey. One evening, they were left stranded in a town in Ukraine, where they knew no one. The sisters were on their own for four years; they never saw their mother again, but finally, with the help of a humanitarian aid group, they were sent to Twin Falls in Idaho.[67]

The world's largest Greek yoghurt factory had just opened in Twin Falls, and the sisters soon found jobs there. Nisa recalled that when she was working one day, she asked a man to move out of her way so she could mop up some water on the floor. 'He looks at me and says, "What is your name? Where did you come from?" When he asked me, I was so full inside I just started crying. He hugged me and asked, "Why you are crying?" I was feeling so emotional. I told him where I came from, how hard was life for us and how I started working here. He said, "Don't worry. You are in a safe place."'[68]

That man was Hamdi Ulukaya, the CEO and founder of Chobani, the multi-billion-dollar yoghurt company.[69] Since founding the company, Ulukaya, who insists he is 'not a businessman', has operated Chobani with several core principles that he called the 'anti-CEO playbook' in a TED Talk in 2019. These principles include accountability, community, gratitude, being accountable to the consumer (as opposed to corporate boards) and responsibility.[70]

Hiring refugees is one way in which Ulukaya cares for his community; by 2019, 30 per cent of Chobani's employees were refugees and immigrants.[71] 'The private sector has a powerful incentive to find new solutions to a crisis that cannot be solved by governments and goodwill alone,' Ulukaya has written.[72] To help mobilize other employers, he also founded a refugee advocacy foundation called the Tent Partnership for Refugees.

An immigrant himself, Ulukaya grew up in a shepherd's village in the Kurd Mountains in Turkey. As a young man in the mid-1990s, he decided to move to New York to study business;[73] by 2005, he had bought a struggling yoghurt plant in a small town called South Edmeston, 200 miles north of Manhattan. The plant was in New York's 'rust belt', a region of once-booming factories that had been dormant and decaying since the 1970s.

Ulukaya had his sights set on bringing higher-quality yoghurt to the US, and within two years the company was producing what is known as 'Greek yoghurt', a product that represented less than 1 per cent of the American yoghurt market at the time.[74] Compared to the competition, it was 'thicker, creamier, less sweet and contained more protein'.[75]

Within five years, Chobani was the most popular Greek yoghurt brand in the country and had revenues of $1 billion.[76] Many credited Chobani with the growth of the Greek yoghurt segment in the country; by 2018 it made up half of the total yoghurt market in the US.[77]

The company has been socially conscious from the start, paying above-market wages and supporting the communities in which it operates. 'Maybe we didn't always call it sustainability, but working this way is who we are,' Ulukaya wrote in a sustainability report in 2019. The report stated that the company's purpose was 'to make universal wellness happen sooner' and outlined the company's five sustainability focus areas: community, operations, people, responsibility and supply chain.[78]

In that 2019 report, Chobani also created nine 'North Star goals' that are 'tangible, trackable, and most importantly, meaningful targets for the business over the next four years'. The goals were designed to be bold, push the company and 'drive innovation'.[79] They include powering its manufacturing operations with 100 per cent renewable energy, achieving water-neutral manufacturing operations, sending zero waste to landfill, running the firm's fleet on renewable fuel, sourcing sustainably, looking after the well-being of dairy workers, using sustainable packaging, achieving inclusion and diversity, and strengthening rural communities through business, philanthropy and development initiatives.[80]

Chobani has already done a lot of work to strengthen rural communities. By 2019, its New York operation had 'contributed to a nearly 50 per cent regional reduction in unemployment' over a five-year period.[81] The company employed more than ten thousand people in the state, and it paid its employees 42 per cent more than the county's median income.[82]

Chobani also launched an equity-sharing program in 2016, after the company had been valued at several billion dollars. Discussing his reasons for sharing his profits, Ulukaya said, 'I've built something I never thought would be such a success, but I cannot think of Chobani being built without all these people.'[83] Employees own 10 per cent of the company.[84]

With the company's many impact-focused initiatives and operational practices, Ulukaya seems intent on using Chobani as a vehicle for making the world a better place. 'For me, life is about building something that makes positive changes in people's lives. This should be the new way of business. If Chobani can lead on this, not only with the product it makes, but the kind of impact it has and the environment it creates, that would be a legacy that I could be proud of.'[85]

While Chobani started with employment impact, Adidas is also beginning to deliver impact by focusing on a particular aspect of its business – in its case, starting with the environmental impact of its products.

Made to be Remade

The 8.3 billion metric tons of plastic that we have ever produced still exists, and roughly three-quarters of it has become plastic waste.[86] And of that gargantuan amount of used plastic, less than 10 per cent has been recycled.[87] If we continue the current trend of producing plastic that ends up in the sea, in 30 years' time it will outweigh fish.[88]

In 2015, Adidas, the world's second-largest sportswear manufacturer, with sales of nearly €22 billion ($24.4 billion), began a collaboration with the environmental organization Parley for the Oceans. The partnership aims to intercept the plastic collected on beaches and coastal communities for re-use, 'spinning the problem into a solution' and creating 'high-performance sportswear'. The collected plastic, mostly bottles, would be shipped to a supplier in Taiwan to create thread from the waste, which would be used in the Adidas x Parley line of products.[89] Each pair of shoes would contain the plastic from 11 bottles.[90]

A year after the collaboration was announced, Adidas created 'the first performance products with recycled ocean plastics', and by 2018 it had made six million pairs of shoes in the Adidas x Parley line. Although this project represents a fraction of the 450 million pairs of shoes the company makes every year,[91] Adidas also announced that 'we have committed ourselves to use only 100 per cent recycled polyester by 2024'.

Of course, even products made from recycled plastic can eventually end up in landfills and the oceans, and this is why Adidas has challenged itself to make products from materials that can be completely re-used. After six years of work, the company announced a running shoe called Loop in 2019, which was 'made to be remade'.[92] Unlike other sneakers, the entire shoe is made of a single material called thermoplastic polyurethane (TPU), and the various pieces are fused together with heat rather than glue. The entire shoe – laces and soles included – can be put into a grinder, which transforms it into pellets, creating raw material for another pair of shoes.[93] The first 200 pairs were given away for beta testing, and sales are slated to begin soon.[94]

Though the ground-up bits of one Loop shoe don't yet equal the materials needed for a new pair, Adidas hopes to reach 'full circularity' – a 1:1 ratio – in the near future.[95] One recycled pair of the first Loop sneakers currently provides 10 per cent of the materials needed for a new shoe.

Both the Parley range and the Loop shoes were developed as part of what the company calls 'Futurecraft'– experimental designs that 'the company openly admits [are] ... minimum viable product[s] that Adidas can generally only produce in limited numbers'.[96] But the company is able to scale these products quickly: Paul Gaudio, global creative director, estimates that they could sell 'tens of millions of Loop shoes within three to five years'.[97]

The Loop shoes' 'circularity' process is still being hammered out – one idea is to sell the shoes with a shipping box and return label, so that when the consumer is finished with them they can simply send them back for a new pair, perhaps using a subscription model.[98] Eric Liedtke, an executive board member, put it this way: 'Our dream is that you can keep wearing the same shoes over and over again.'[99]

People debate whether companies like Adidas that focus on a single impact dimension can deliver significant positive impact. While it is true that a company can deliver welcome impact through one dimension of its activities only, it can simultaneously continue to create negative impact through others. For this reason, it is fundamental that companies aim to generate as great a *net* positive impact as possible across all their activities. IKEA is one company that tries to do that.

Living Within the Limits of the Planet

By 2018, IKEA had 422 stores in more than 50 markets and was generating revenues of nearly €39 billion ($43.3 billion).[100] It also uses 1 per cent of the entire world's lumber supply.[101] The retailer's global position and ability to make an impact was not lost on company executives: 'Through our size and reach we have the opportunity to inspire and enable more than one billion people to live better lives, within the limits of the planet,' said Torbjörn Lööf, the CEO of Inter IKEA Group, which owns the IKEA brand.[102] Jesper Brodin, the CEO of Ingka Group, which owns and operates multiple franchises under the umbrella IKEA brand, said the company was committed to sustainability for three key reasons: because customers were demanding it, because being responsible with scarce resources was a matter of survival and 'because we believe this is the right thing to do'.[103]

IKEA's sustainability strategy, known as 'People and Planet Positive', was launched in 2012. In 2018, the company updated this strategy to align with the SDGs and focus on three areas: 'healthy and sustainable living', 'circular and climate-positive' and creating a 'fair and equal' society, starting with those in the company's value chain.[104] Its targets include phasing out virgin fossil-based plastic from its products by 2020 and using only renewable or recyclable materials by 2030. And the company is making good progress towards those targets: by 2018, 60 per cent of its products were of renewable materials, 10 per cent were made from recycled materials, and all of its cotton and 85 per cent of its wood was from sustainable sources.[105]

The company has estimated that of its total greenhouse gas emissions, the top two contributors were its operations associated with raw materials (38 per cent) and customers' product use (23 per cent).[106] While IKEA is known all over the world for affordable furniture, it also has another reputation: 'that its products are disposable rather than hard-wearing' and that they soon end up in landfill.[107] In the US alone, every year people throw away an estimated 9.7 million tons of furniture that ends up in landfill,[108] the equivalent weight of over 7 million small cars.[109]

To combat this unsustainability, IKEA has committed to attaining 100 per cent 'circularity' in its operations by 2030. This means designing 'all products from the very beginning to be repurposed, repaired, reused, resold and recycled', said IKEA sustainability chief Lena Pripp-Kovac.[110]

It also means changing consumer behavior. 'We need to address the elephant in the room, which is unsustainable consumption,' Andreas Ahrens, the company's head of climate, said in 2019.[111] That is why, in 'a radical departure from its traditional business model', the company began piloting furniture leasing in Switzerland in 2019, stating that it could blaze a trail for 'scalable subscription services'.[112] After a furniture lease was over, consumers might choose something else and IKEA would be able to refurbish the returned goods 'prolonging the lifecycle of the products'.[113]

Initiatives like these are moving IKEA toward its goal of decreasing its carbon footprint by 15 per cent. That goal is more ambitious than it sounds: taking growth projections into account, it requires reducing the carbon footprint of each product by 70 per cent by 2030. The company also has plans to introduce spare parts, which would allow consumers to prolong the life of discontinued products, and it has already started recycling programs for large items like mattresses in some countries.[114]

Another way IKEA is helping its customers lead more sustainable lives is through its product design – such as a couch that can be more easily separated into recycled parts,[115] curtains that help clean the air,[116] and low-energy and water-saving appliances.[117] The company also now only sells LED lightbulbs (which last up to 15 times longer than incandescent bulbs and can use 85 per cent less energy). Walk into an IKEA showroom today and you will see many products made from recycled materials, such as baskets made from recycled PET bottles, rugs made from scraps of linen and spray bottles made from the protective film that is used to cover furniture.[118]

Impact is also beginning to affect the company's logistics operations. IKEA aims to 'fully decarbonize its delivery fleet', starting in Amsterdam, Los Angeles, New York, Paris and Shanghai. As Jesper Brodin puts it, 'Climate change is no longer just a threat – it's a reality.' Retailers of products designed for mass consumption 'will simply not be around unless you have a business model that harmonizes with the resources of this planet. There's no contradiction between this ambition and our business ambition.'[119]

These views are becoming mainstream. For example, Mark Carney, the former Governor of the Bank of England who was responsible for the financial stability of the banking system in the UK, urged companies to bring climate risk into their decision-making and to disclose their environmental impact comprehensively. The Task Force on Climate-Related Financial Disclosures (TCFD), which Carney established in 2015, has attracted over one thousand signatories, including companies in chemicals, energy and transport that are responsible for considerable carbon emissions.

It is clear that companies like IKEA want to have a positive impact on the world, but how do you quantify and compare that impact? How can you tell when an IKEA, Adidas, Danone or Chobani reaches the point of doing more good than harm to society and the environment?

The Watershed:
Impact-Weighted Accounts

It is a basic management principle that you can't manage what you don't measure. Accurate data and reliable measurement are essential to achieving real change because they create transparency, authenticity and trust. This is why standardized impact measurement is so important. It makes it possible for impact to take its rightful place alongside profit by enabling us to arrive at a company's net impact, or putting it in other words, its *social and environmental* bottom line.

The work around impact metrics and the valuation of impact has, until now, stopped short of providing a system for measuring and comparing the real net impact created by companies, but useful progress has been made. B Lab is probably the best framework available for businesses to measure and communicate about their impact. Founded in 2006 by Jay

Coen Gilbert, Bart Houlahan and Andrew Kassoy, B Lab is a non-profit dedicated to 'using business as a force for good'.[120] It has created the Global Impact Investing Rating System (GIIRS) to measure the impact of all stakeholders, including workers, customers and communities.[121]

Other efforts include that of the Global Impact Investing Network (GIIN), founded in 2009, which provides a catalogue of standardized performance metrics for businesses receiving impact investment capital.

> It is a basic management principle that you can't manage what you don't measure

The Sustainability Accounting Standards Board (SASB), founded in 2011, focuses on serving the needs of investors – SASB standards measure the impact of businesses across a range of issues relating to sustainability. The Global Reporting Initiative's (GRI) Sustainability Reporting Standards, first launched in 2000, focus on sustainability, transparency and corporate disclosure, rather than on impact measurement. Other measurement initiatives include those of the World Benchmarking Alliance and the World Economic Forum's International Business Council, which both seek to assess companies' performance in contributing towards the UN's Sustainable Development Goals (SDGs).

But these efforts are still early steps in our journey to a standardized, comprehensive system of impact measurement. If investors and the companies in which they invest are to make decisions that take impact into account properly, they will require accounts that express *both* the profits *and* the impact that a company makes through its products, employment and operations, preferably within the familiar framework of regular financial accounts.

That is why the Impact-Weighted Accounts Initiative (IWAI) incubated at Harvard Business School is so important. Launched in 2019, it is a research-led joint initiative of the Global Steering Group (GSG) and the Impact Management Project (IMP). Under the leadership of professor George Serafeim, it is building a framework for financial accounts that integrate the impact a company creates. This ground-breaking initiative brings together academics, practitioners, companies and investors and seeks to build on all impact measurement work that has been done to date.

To arrive at impact-weighted accounts, it is necessary to give a monetary value to the social and environmental impacts created by businesses. This monetization of impact pushes portfolio theory to the next level, allowing investors to optimize risk–return–impact in the same way that they already optimize risk and return.

But how will impact-weighted accounts work? They will apply impact coefficients to the various lines of a company's profit and loss statement – sales, employment costs, cost of goods sold – to arrive at an impact-weighted profit line, which reflects the impact a company has on the environment, on the people it employs directly and within its supply chain, and on its consumers. They will similarly apply weighting to the assets that appear on a company's balance sheet.

These impact coefficients would be set by an impact accounting board, similar to the ones we already have for financial accounting. This board would establish 'generally accepted impact principles' (GAIP), to sit alongside the 'generally accepted accounting principles' (GAAP) we use in financial accounting. GAIPs will make it possible for companies to publish impact-weighted accounts in the same form as their financial ones, allowing us to judge impact *and* profit in a familiar way when making decisions.

By monetizing the impact that companies have on people and the environment, the IWAI enables rigorous comparison between companies. This comparison will influence consumers, investors and employees, and ultimately affect a company's value. The end result will be huge, a transformational change in capital flows, as our money starts to move throughout our whole system in search of impact.

Let's take a look at the environmental impact of companies. The IWAI's sample currently contains over three thousand five hundred companies. Calculating monetary estimates of the environmental impacts of these companies on the basis of publicly available data provides interesting insights. For instance, Coca-Cola and PepsiCo historically had a corporate rivalry, yet they display noticeably different environmental footprints (the effect a company's operations have on the environment).

In 2018, PepsiCo's sales ($64.7 billion) were twice Coca-Cola's ($31.8 billion), yet PepsiCo's estimated annual environmental cost was $1.8 billion, much less than Coca-Cola's $3.7 billion.[122] This drastic difference in environmental efficiency can be attributed mainly to the two companies' differing behavior around water usage: Coca-Cola withdrew about three and a half times more water than PepsiCo in 2018 yet discharged much less, resulting in total water use of about five times the volume of PepsiCo's. Despite the fact that Coca-Cola generated half of PepsiCo's revenue in 2018, its impact through water use alone resulted in an environmental cost of $2 billion, whereas the environmental cost of PepsiCo's water use was around $408 million.[123] This example shows how measurement can shed light on the true performance of companies.

Another interesting comparison is the difference between the environmental costs arising from the operations of Exxon Mobil, Royal Dutch Shell and BP (not taking into account the environmental cost of their products). While Exxon Mobil's revenue in 2018 was $279 billion, its environmental cost was estimated to be around $38 billion. In comparison, Shell's revenue in the same year was $330 billion with an environmental cost of $22 billion. BP had an annual revenue of $225 billion and an environmental cost of $13 billion. Exxon Mobil stands out, therefore, as the least environmentally efficient of the three rivals with an environmental intensity (environmental cost/revenue) of 13.6% vs 6.7% and 5.8% respectively. This is largely due to the substantial cost of Exxon's greenhouse gas emissions; at about $40 billion they were roughly one and a half times higher than Shell's emissions and almost two and a half times greater than BP's. Exxon also had the highest sulphur oxide discharge and water withdrawal volume of the three companies.[124]

Looking at the environmental effect of greenhouse gas emissions from the operations of car companies, the environmental damage caused by Ford amounts to $1.5 billion, which represents 1 per cent of its sales revenue. When we compare this with other car companies of a similar size, we see that the environmental damage caused by General Motors amounts to $2 billion, representing 1.4 per cent of its revenue, while the damage caused by Daimler AG, commonly known as Mercedes, amounts to $1 billion, representing 0.5 per cent of its revenue.

In other words, for every $100 of its sales in 2017, Ford's emissions of greenhouse gases from its operations caused $1 of environmental damage, General Motors' caused $1.40 and Daimler AG's caused $0.50.[125]

Measuring operational impact in this way reveals insights about each company's performance. Due to the lack of public effort to monetize corporate-level impacts so far, investors have been unaware of how companies are really performing environmentally. Impact-weighted accounts that allow everyone to see the cost of environmental impacts, and make comparisons across companies and industries, enable accurate analysis. This is the key to reducing the environmental damage caused by companies and achieving our environmental goals.

Companies don't just create environmental impact through their operations, they also create it through their products. If we continue with examples from the automobile industry, and take Ford as a case study, the emissions from Ford's cars can be calculated using publicly available data. Using Ford's tailpipe emissions, their annual sales of nearly six million passenger vehicles (cars and lightweight small trucks), the assumption that these vehicles stay on the road for a year and drive the average annual US mileage of ~13,000 miles a year, combined with the social cost of carbon at around $300 per ton, the environmental cost of emissions from one year's sales of Ford passenger vehicles is estimated at $8.8 billion a year.[126]

The impact of a company's products can be monetized across a number of other dimensions, such as quality, accessibility and recyclability. One component of quality is a product's effectiveness. For a food company like General Mills, the effectiveness of their products is reflected in the nutritional profile of their products – how healthy they are for the consumer. Using publicly available data, it is estimated that the company creates $698 million in value from the wholegrain content of the products it sells and $639 million in costs from its products' trans fat content, creating a net positive impact of $59 million. These figures are calculated using three elements: the wholegrain and trans fat content of the company's products,[127] its sales data[128] and the recommended levels of annual individual consumption.[129]

Assuming that the consumption of wholegrain is associated with a 17 per cent decrease in risk of developing coronary heart disease, the consumption of trans fat is associated with a 23 per cent increase in the risk of developing it, and the prevalence of CHD is 5.23% in the United States,[130] the medical and productivity costs associated with coronary heart disease can be used to identify the net value created by General Mills through this element of their products' nutritional profile. Similar estimates can be calculated for the value or costs of other nutrients in products that are associated with an increase or decrease in the risk of contracting various diseases, such as salt, added sugar or fiber.

The companies that are reacting to major industry trends by making the most radical changes to their products' impact are most likely to enjoy a clear increase in interest from consumers and investors. Impact-weighted accounts create a 'race to the top' among rival companies, which both improves the well-being of our population and reduces the damage to the environment.

Until now, the prevailing view has been that impact cannot be measured reliably enough to be really useful. However, in the words of John Maynard Keynes, 'It is better to be roughly right than precisely wrong.' We do not require 100 per cent accuracy in our measurement of impact. Risk thinking did not require 100 per cent accuracy either – it only required dependable accuracy. In the words of professor George Serafeim, impact measurement 'should happen, can happen and is already happening'. The evidence in the examples above make that clear.

It also shows why it is not sufficient to just measure some specific impacts which companies create. In order for investors and others to make intelligent choices, we need to measure all the key impacts a company creates, put a value on them and reflect this value through their financial accounts. Once we start doing so, we will have plenty of scope to refine our impact accounting system over time, as we have done with our financial accounting system. Framing and implementing Generally Accepted Impact Principles (GAIP) will take time, but we must remember that the financial accounts we use today have taken nearly a century to refine. Every journey starts with a single step.

Some might point out that impact-weighted accounts will involve judgement calls in how we design the underlying accounting treatment. That is true, but it is important to recognize that this is also true for our financial accounts. Take the recent decision in Generally Accepted Accounting Principles in the US to change the treatment of leases. This decision, based on a judgement, has had huge consequences for companies' balance sheets. We should not be afraid of making judgements.

When investors are able to look at impact-weighted accounts, they will start to compare companies' financial and impact performance at the same time. Financial analysts will begin to search for a correlation between companies' impact, growth and profit, and money will flow to those businesses that do the best job of optimizing risk–return–impact, bringing about a significant change in the general behavior of companies.

Even the less comprehensive ESG disclosures are affecting the value of companies. In a recent interview with the Financial Times, Savita Subramanian, head of US equity and quantitative strategy at Bank of America, recently said that the best signal of risks to companies' future earnings is ESG data and that 'Traditional financial metrics, such as earnings quality, leverage and profitability don't come close to ESG metrics as a signal of future earnings risk or volatility in earnings'. The same article went on to say that investment managers are beginning to recognize that 'companies with similar fundamental characteristics in the same stock market sector can receive markedly different valuations depending on the quality of their ESG disclosures.'[131]

When the IWAI, or a similar initiative, brings us a framework to quantify impact in a way investors can rely on, the game will change even more. Companies' impact will greatly influence the capital, talent and consumers they attract.

Businesses that do not deliver both an attractive financial performance and equally impressive impact will be overtaken by new competitors. They will become the Blockbuster Video or Kodak of their day and be at risk of disappearing because they are too slow to adapt to a changing world. This is how this new accounting method will drive new and impactful solutions to our biggest social and environmental challenges.

By incentivizing companies to deliver impact so that they can maximize their impact-weighted profit, impact-weighted accounts will help to reduce economic inequality and preserve the environment. Companies will be incentivized to develop products that provide better value for money, serve underserved communities, reduce negative and create positive impact on the environment. They will be incentivized to improve employment conditions, retrain their workers, pay proper wages, employ individuals who are usually excluded from the workforce, and maintain gender and ethnic diversity. In sum, the use of impact-weighted accounts will establish new norms of behavior in business.

Imagine businesses actively improving their environmental footprint: reducing their emissions, limiting their water usage, launching healthier food products, and developing more effective and affordable medicines. The possibilities are endless.

Such a change is not a fantasy – it has, in fact, happened before. Immediately after the Wall Street Crash in 1929, people asked how investors could possibly have been able to decide which companies to invest in when each one picked its own accounting firm and accounting policies, and there were no auditors. At the time, some business leaders argued that the introduction of the proposed US Securities Exchange Commission, generally accepted accounting principles and auditors would be the end of the American capitalist system; looking back, we wonder how previous generations were able to invest for so long without any dependable information about the profitability of companies. The same will one day be true of impact-weighted accounts.

Businesses that lack impact integrity will run the risk of losing customers, investors and talented employees

When companies become convinced that impact-weighted accounts are on the way, they will begin to collect the data necessary to calculate and manage their impact. The transition from our existing system to one that creates positive impact will involve some cost, but, as I like to say, principles might have a cost but are always a bargain in the end. Businesses that lack impact integrity will run the risk of losing customers, investors and talented employees. To quote Warren Buffet, 'It's only when the tide goes out, that you learn who's been swimming naked.'[132] Once the tide goes out and impact-weighted accounts are in common use, everyone will be astonished that companies were ever able to make decisions based on profit alone.

Chapter 5

THE DAWN OF IMPACT PHILANTHROPY

We must shift all our resources to achieving outcomes

As we have just seen, impact measurement is the key to delivering positive impact through business, but it is also the key to unlocking philanthropy's full potential. Here is why.

Some 25,000 businesses in the US reached $50 million in sales over a period of 25 years, but only 144 non-profits managed to do so.[1] Why? Of the 1.5 million registered non-profits in the US, only 5 per cent have revenues over $10 million per year. Why are so many charitable organizations doing good work on a small scale? Think of the impact that a $50 or $500 million charity can have on the communities it helps – why have so few non-profits managed to reach that kind of scale? The main reason is our philanthropic model, which impact thinking is starting to change.

In order to understand the change that impact is bringing, we first must examine how and why philanthropy has unwittingly kept most non-profits small. The lack of a common system for measuring impact has affected the way in which money has traditionally been given away. Until recently, philanthropy revolved solely around gifts and grants. Most foundations have felt that the appropriate way to help the disadvantaged is through charity, which translates into giving out grants to fund activities without rigorously measuring the outcomes created.

Over the last century, charitable foundations established by wealthy individuals and families have grown considerably and become institutionalized. In the process, they have developed some unhelpful habits. For example, because they have relied on a very qualitative form of reporting about the outcomes achieved by their grants, many foundations have tried to spread their money widely, making small grants for relatively short periods. They will give grants to charitable service providers for two or three years, before moving on to help another organization. After all, if you don't really know what good you're accomplishing with your money, it is hard to have the conviction to fund any single organization for the long term. Then, in the absence of rigorous impact measurement, most foundations require their grantees to spend as little as possible on overheads, in order to ensure that as much money as possible goes to those in need.

The end result is that the vast majority of the non-profit delivery organizations they fund remain small and cash-strapped. Of the more than 5,400 non-profit organizations in the US that responded to the latest State of the Non-Profit

Sector Survey, conducted by the Non-Profit Finance Fund which is led by Antony Bugg-Levine, more than three-quarters had seen increased demand for their services, but more than half were unable to meet that demand – and the two previous years showed the same result.[2] If businesses see increasing demand, they sell more product, make more money, invest and keep on growing. But when non-profits see increasing demand, they have to turn struggling people away. And they often don't have access to the money they need to grow, because their funders have already moved on to the next grantee.

When you are struggling to stay afloat, you can't afford to take risks. Most non-profits can't experiment with new solutions to social problems. Experimentation inevitably means occasional failure, which scares off donors. As a result, most charities are forced to live from hand to mouth, unable to engage in long-term thinking about their growth and performance. The pressure to drive down overheads prevents them from paying competitive salaries to attract the top talent – except when self-sacrificing, talented individuals are willing to work for less.

> The inability to measure impact is at the root of all these problems

The inability to measure impact is at the root of all these problems.[3] Many people who work in the charitable sector or in purpose-driven businesses believe that measurement is too cumbersome and expensive to be practical for small, cash-strapped organizations. Some believe that measuring impact would unhelpfully disrupt the status quo, and many are uncomfortable with the idea of philanthropists evaluating the performance of non-profits and investing in the top performers. However, what they don't see is that the current model of philanthropy leads to huge inefficiencies and often drives organizations to focus on securing grants rather than on delivering impact.

Without measuring impact, philanthropy cannot ensure that delivery organizations get the large sums of money they need to tackle the great challenges we face. By relying on impact measurement, philanthropy can deploy grants more effectively, attract investment from the private sector and motivate delivery organizations to innovate and scale. Impact investors want to see measurable financial and impact returns. They want the organizations they invest in to take risks and reach new ambitious levels of performance and growth. And today, thanks to some exciting breakthroughs, collaboration between foundations and investors, governments and non-profits enables philanthropy to adapt some of businesses' best tools – and use them to make the biggest possible impact on society and the environment.

Social Impact Bonds: The Catalyst

Impact philanthropy, which takes many forms, offers a new alternative to conventional grant-making. The most prominent catalyst of these new approaches is the Social Impact Bond (SIB). When the first one was introduced in 2010, it turned conventional philanthropic wisdom on its head. The SIB demonstrated that it was possible to link the funding of a project to its impact on society. By doing so, it was able to attract private capital to scale the efforts of charitable organizations. It also allowed governments and philanthropists to pay for results after they had been achieved rather than put their money at risk upfront.

As we saw in our discussion of the SIB in Chapter 1, it brings together three key players: investors, outcome payers and service providers. In this set-up, philanthropists can play two possible roles: that of investor or outcome payer. When they provide upfront funding as investors, they get their capital back and earn a financial return on their investment if the program meets its goals. In the worst-case scenario, when the social benefit is not achieved, the philanthropists lose their investment (and, in essence, they can view this investment loss as a donation). When they commit to being an outcome payer, they pay only when outcomes have been successfully achieved, shifting the delivery risk from themselves to the investors.

A SIB is an effective addition to traditional grants for two reasons: when philanthropists play the role of the investor, it pays them back and provides more money for future grant-making; when they play the role of an outcome payer, it ties their philanthropic funding to paying for targeted outcomes once they have been achieved – and this generates focus and dynamism among delivery organizations in achieving desired outcomes.

As we will see in the next chapter, at the moment governments are most frequently the party that pays back the investors in the SIB model, which makes sense because they benefit from the cost savings or additional revenues achieved by SIB programs. However, philanthropists have a big role to play as outcome payers themselves and in drawing governments to become outcome payers, by participating alongside them.

There are a few reasons why philanthropists are increasingly excited by the potential of SIBs to deliver real impact. Most importantly, they bring about many critical improvements in service delivery. Let's revisit the inaugural Peterborough SIB from Chapter 1.

The problem at hand was the rate at which offenders reoffended after being released from prison. The Peterborough SIB provided £5 million ($6.65 million) to six non-profit organizations, which collectively called themselves the 'One Service'. In the past, each of them had focused on a different part of the rehabilitation process, but none of them had been responsible for reducing recidivism.

For the first time, they now worked together to understand and tackle the root causes. What happens to people after their release from prison became a lot clearer: 40 per cent didn't know where they would be sleeping, 25 per cent faced challenges related to addiction, and 39 per cent didn't have enough money to make it to their first unemployment benefit payment or a new job.[4] For many, when they got out, the only money they had in their pockets was the statutory 'discharge grant' of £46 ($61).[5] No wonder drug dealers waiting at the gates to offer them a place to stay, and something to help them forget prison, brought them straight back to a life of crime.

By joining together, these delivery organizations could concentrate on rehabilitating released prisoners through a multi-pronged approach that focused on their collective impact rather than on their individual activities. The result was a massive breakthrough: by the end of the second year of the Peterborough SIB, the project had reduced recidivism by 11 per cent, at a time when the UK as a whole experienced a national increase of 10 per cent.[6]

SIBs Take Off

The success of the Peterborough SIB was a decisive achievement that caused discussion about the future direction of philanthropy. The market for SIBs and DIBs has attracted over $400 million in investment,[7] and more than $1 billion of commitments to pay for successful social outcomes involving children, youth, employment, social welfare, criminal justice, education and healthcare. SIBs are showing that they can deliver a better execution and expansion of social services. They are also proving something which many have long believed: that prevention is a lot cheaper and more effective than cure. Preventative interventions through SIBs are proving successful in addressing many social challenges, from recidivism and homelessness to teenage unemployment and diabetes.

SIBs and DIBs are spreading across the world. The UK is still a major center for SIB innovation, with its 67 SIBs representing nearly 40 per cent of the global total.[8] The United States is also a major hub of activity, with 25 active SIBs. The Netherlands has eleven, followed by Australia with ten; France has six; Canada five; Japan, Israel, India, Germany and Belgium have three each; Finland, New Zealand and South Korea have two each;

and Austria, Russia, Colombia, Peru, Sweden, Switzerland and Argentina have one each.[9]

As the SIB market expands, philanthropists, governments and investors are becoming more aware of its potential. SIB funds are appearing on the scene and starting to show what they can achieve. In the UK, Bridges Fund Management raised the first two social impact bond funds in the world, in 2013 and 2019. With a combined value of £60 million ($79.8 million),[10] these funds, which include institutional investors and charitable foundations, have put together a diverse portfolio of 40 SIBs that support more than 90 social service providers in delivering better outcomes in children's services, education and homelessness.[11] The £25 million ($33.25 million) invested so far is due to deliver over £150 million worth of outcomes for government,[12] with a projected net annual return of about 5 per cent to investors. In other words, impact bonds pay benefits to government, returns to investors and create better outcomes for society.

Local government is now often driving the growth of SIBs. This is particularly true in the UK, where government officials view SIBs as 'social outcome contracts'. Unlike traditional contracts, where you pay along the way for services, in a social outcome contract you pay at the end, when results have been achieved. Local government officials are realizing that this represents a better way of delivering social services. This is because the SIB brings discipline in delivering results, generates data on how best to deliver those results, and provides transparency about the effectiveness of a program – all of which is highly valuable to governments, as well as philanthropists and social service providers.

Success stories abound. In the UK, the Bridges Ways to Wellness SIB, for example, was commissioned by the National Health Service in 2014. The aim was to help adults with multiple long-term health conditions, such as diabetes, and heart problems, change their lifestyle through a 'social prescribing' service and thus improve their health. Doctors had long struggled to make a real difference for such patients, where the solution needed was a social rather than a medical one. This new service helped people to exercise, reduce their isolation and improve their diet, allowing them to avoid hospital treatment and thus saving money for the government. The project has beaten all of its targets, helping over five thousand adults to improve their health and delivering a 35 per cent reduction in healthcare costs.[13]

The Fusion Housing SIB, which tackled youth homelessness in the UK, is another demonstration of SIB success. The three-year program, which launched in 2015, raised just under £1 million ($1.33 million) for Fusion and a number of other charitable service providers to implement an outcome-based program to reduce and prevent homelessness.[14]

Although Tasha Dyson, the head of housing services at Fusion Housing, was initially hesitant about the outcome-based approach, she quickly recognized its value: 'Running an outcome-based contract with very vulnerable young people seemed like a recipe for disaster, to be quite honest. However, I am eating my words – it is actually the best way to support vulnerable young people because it allows flexibility of delivery.'

The focus on measurement required in an outcome-based contracting approach was new to those delivering services on the ground. Helen Minett, director of Fusion Housing, said, 'I have to admit I was dragged into the world of statistical analysis kicking and screaming. But I now absolutely understand the benefits of it, not only in evidencing what we're doing but in making a difference in how we move forward.'[15]

Fusion's success persuaded the local government officials at Kirklees Council of the power of this new mechanism to help local people; as a result, they used its outcome-based approach to redesign one of their existing contracts to provide housing services for vulnerable adults more effectively.

In a further indication of the increasing belief in SIBs, a successful £2.5 million ($3.3 million) pilot program helping people at risk of homelessness originally launched by central government was scaled up by Kirklees to a £23 million ($30.6 million) contract.[16]

In the US, Maycomb Capital, an impact investment manager co-founded by Goldman Sachs alumna, Andi Phillips, has launched the first American equivalent of the Bridges SIB Funds. The fund, which was launched in 2018, aims to raise a total of $50 million and includes Prudential Financial, the Kresge Foundation and Steve Ballmer, the former CEO of Microsoft, among its backers.[17] One of Maycomb's investments is in the Massachusetts Pathways to Economic Advancement SIB, which was launched in 2017 by Social Finance US to focus on integrating immigrants into society.

The Greater Boston area is home to a significant refugee and immigrant population that has little or no English skills. This makes it hard for them to get jobs, especially higher-paying ones, and this population earns $24,000 less on average per year than immigrants with similar credentials who are fluent in English. Many of them are left dependent on state help, with over 50 per cent relying on cash assistance.[18]

Part of the reason for this situation is the lack of language learning services, with at least 16,000 adult learners on waiting lists. On top of this, the learning programs that are available are not complemented by help in transitioning to a job or higher salary.[19] There was a clear need to achieve more effective results at scale, and the pay-for-outcomes model allowed this to happen.

Through Pathways, 40 investors provided $12.43 million upfront, to enable the charitable service provider – Jewish Vocational Services (JVS) – to serve two thousand English language learners through four programs that combine language lessons and employment services.[20] The goal of the project is to increase employment, secure higher-wage jobs and achieve a successful transition to higher education. Project outcomes are measured quarterly and dictate the payments received by investors. So far, eight success payments have been made.[21]

Jerry Rubin, the JVS CEO, explains what this means for the charitable service provider: 'When you are literally paid for success, it drives program quality. If you're measuring wage gains, which is possible, your program design will result in people getting better jobs and increased wages. Right now, adult education and workforce development are separate. This model merges the two. The reason you want to merge them is that's what people want and need. This model produces genuinely meaningful outcomes for both the clients and the Commonwealth, which is transformative.'[22]

Part of the reason JVS got involved in the pay-for-outcomes program model was because they wanted to expand their activity to the large numbers of adults that could benefit from their services, but as Jerry Rubin stated, 'we have no financing mechanism'. Another reason was that this model allowed them to offer a service that was designed to achieve better outcomes – in this case, better economic opportunity – by providing a combination of English language instruction, employment services and career coaching.[23]

In other words, the combination of investor discipline and pay-for-outcomes equals expansion, innovation and impact. When you consider how difficult it is for these service providers to secure grants, it is clear that pay-for-outcomes offers a much more effective funding option for those who wish to attract substantial capital in order to scale.

As of January 2020, there were 26 active SIB projects in the US[24] and many others in development. And the total amount raised is greater than in the UK – as always in finance, the US is scaling fastest.

But as with anything new, there are growing pains and challenges. So far, most SIBs are quite small: the median number of beneficiaries of each of them is around 600, with a median upfront capital commitment of only around £2 million ($2.7 million).[25] The largest SIB in the world, which supports teenage mothers in South Carolina, is still only $30 million.

SIBs are more complicated to design and implement than grants, as they involve three stakeholders: the outcome payer, the delivery organization and the investor. This is currently leading to higher transaction costs relative to capital deployed, but the ease and speed of implementation are improving all the time. As experience grows, terms and outcome metrics will standardize, and both professional outcome funds and SIB/DIB investment funds will enter the market and allow impact bonds to scale. SIBs and DIBs should ultimately be judged according to the cost per successful outcome and the number of successful outcomes they can achieve, both of which I expect to be significantly more favorable than can be achieved through a traditional grant.

The ultimate goal is to help more people and solve bigger problems

With the arrival of what we call 'impact philanthropy', the best service providers are keeping data on their outcomes as well as their activities. This is critical, because tracking outcomes makes pay-for-success investment models such as SIBs and DIBs accessible. If service providers can accurately track the outcomes of their interventions, it will become easier for them to attract investment capital. The ultimate goal is to help more people and solve bigger problems – giving social service providers the tools and the money they need to innovate and grow is the way to do it.

DIBs: A New Model for Philanthropy and Aid

In the original SIB model, private investors put up the cash and governments paid them for success. However, in most developing economies governments lack the money to pay. In a development impact bond (DIB), foundations and aid organizations step in to pay for outcomes, alongside the governments of emerging countries.

There are plenty of urgent outcomes to achieve in emerging markets, but there is one big catch: money. Achieving the SDG goals by 2030 requires us to find about $30 trillion.[26] Traditional models of philanthropic giving and government spending just aren't going to cut it.

DIBs offer an innovative way to tackle important problems in education, health and the environment that blight lives and constrain economic growth. They can deliver attractive returns, and so can help plug the SDG funding gap. Where governments of emerging countries are unable to pay on their own to achieve the desired outcomes, DIBs are able to attract philanthropy and aid to pay for the outcomes achieved, and to provide investment for the delivery organizations that will achieve them. While many philanthropic donors may consider it futile to just throw money at issues in emerging markets, they are attracted by the idea of paying for outcomes. This is because they get what they pay for, while creating a similar dynamic to the successful one which exists between venture capitalists and entrepreneurs.

In 2015, the first DIB was launched, which aimed to increase girls' access to education in India. Indian children face significant barriers to a proper education: 47 per cent of fifth graders cannot read a paragraph, and 30 per cent cannot do a simple subtraction sum. Familial and cultural expectations make the problem even more severe for girls: 42 per cent of them are told to quit school by their parents, and only 55 per cent of schools in the country have girls' toilets.[27] In the Indian state of Rajasthan, 40 per cent of girls drop out of school before fifth grade.[28]

Narayani had been out of school for several years when Educate Girls, the DIB service provider founded and led by Safeena Husain, stepped in. Educate Girls spent time with her family and convinced them to re-enroll her in fourth grade. Getting back into school for the first time in years was overwhelming, but Educate Girls helped her to do it through a program which involves working with families as well as teachers. The program intervenes with remedial education and support to help girls like Narayani get up to grade level so they'll stay in school.

During the DIB, Educate Girls collected enough data on children's learning styles to revamp their remedial curriculum. Thanks to this intensive work, after two years in the program Narayani can read stories in Hindi, solve math problems and is learning the English alphabet.

The world's first DIB, which was put together by Instiglio, the Colombia-founded impact finance advisor, was a success: the project achieved 92 per cent student enrol-ment, smashing its target of 79 per cent,[29] and 160 per cent of the final learning target.[30] This success translated into success for the investor; UBS Optimus Fund recouped its initial funding of $270,000 from the outcome payer, the Children's Investment Fund Foundation, plus $144,085 rep-resenting a 15 per cent annual return – money that will be reinvested in further programs.[31]

As a result of its success with this tiny DIB, Educate Girls has been able to raise more than $90 million of philanthropic grants to roll out its programs – a huge increase from its initial funding and clear evidence of how DIBs can help charitable service providers to scale.

There are a dozen DIBs in operation today,[32] including the first humanitarian one – the $25 million International Committee of the Red Cross Program for Humanitarian Impact Investment (PHII),[33] with even more in development. In the case of the Red Cross bond, institutional and private investors put up the money needed to establish centers in Mali, Nigeria and the Democratic Republic of Congo, in order to support those injured by violent conflict, accident or disease. An international group of outcome payers (the overseas development agencies of Switzerland, Belgium, the UK and Italy, as well as La Caixa Foundation, a large Spanish banking foundation) will repay investors after five years. Depending on the results, the investors will either earn as much as 7 per cent return each year, or lose up to 40 per cent of their investment.

Under the leadership of Peter Maurer, its President, the Red Cross is seeking to use SIBs and DIBs to reduce its 80 per cent dependency on government grants. 'For many years now, the ICRC has been looking for new funding from governments that do not yet provide support – private sources and innovative funding arrangements,' said Tobias Epprecht, the official in charge of the bond. 'This is an important learning experience for us. If it works, it will be a stepping stone to larger projects.'[34] In other words, DIBs have the potential to create important new revenue streams for charitable delivery organizations like the Red Cross.

These new models undoubtedly have tremendous potential, but as the Educate Girls example shows, the first SIBs and DIBs have started out small. The Educate Girls program targeted a few hundred girls in one state in India. The results were transformative for those who participated, but there are millions more who need the same kind of help.

The Education Commission's 2017 report signals that we face an urgent global learning crisis: 250 million children are not in school, and a further 330 million are not actually learning. If we continue on this trajectory, half of the world's youth will be out of education or failing to learn by 2030, and only one in ten young people in low-income countries will gain basic secondary-level skills.[35] That is a huge problem, and one that can't be solved a couple of hundred kids at a time. To solve problems of this size, large scale pay-for-outcomes models are needed.

Time to Scale Outcome Funds

This is where Outcome Funds come in. These funds are professionally managed vehicles that sign outcome-based contracts with social delivery organizations. Their goal is to scale outcome-based contracts and to drastically reduce the time and cost it takes to put them in place.

Once a contract between a delivery organization and an Outcome Fund has been signed, the delivery organization can raise the investment capital it needs in order to fulfill the contract. This capital can be provided by investors through DIB funds. They might be regular investors, the investment arms of development aid organizations or philanthropic foundations. You can view DIB funds and outcome funds as the two electrodes of a battery, powering the funding of delivery organizations. DIB funds pay the upfront money, while outcome funds pay when the outcomes have been achieved.

This innovative approach is illustrated in the diagram below:

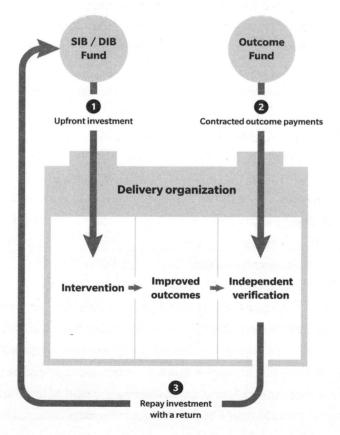

The Role of Outcome Funds in Financing Delivery Organizations

To set up this dynamic, in improving education in emerging countries for example, we go through the following steps:

1. The outcome funders commit USD $1 billion to the Outcome Fund, which signs outcome contracts with delivery organizations

2. This catalyzes up to USD $700 million from investors who finance the social delivery organizations, through DIB funds, to deliver their interventions

3. NGOs and purpose-driven businesses deliver the education interventions to improve learning outcomes

4. Students experience increased educational attainment which is independently verified

5. Achievement of the contracted outcomes triggers payments from the Outcome Fund to repay investors the original investment with a return that increases with the degree of success.

For example, the Education Outcomes Fund for Africa and the Middle East (EOF) aims to raise $1 billion to improve the education of ten million children. It is a joint initiative between the GSG and the Education Commission, which Gordon Brown chairs, and is supported by an international group of foundations looking for innovative ways to maximize improvement in education in Africa and the Middle East, notably the Aliko Dangote Foundation, Ford, Omidyar, The Big Win, ELMA,

UBS Optimus, Hewlett and DFID. Led by Dr Amel Karboul, a former Tunisian government minister, the EOF will help catalyze investment in effective education delivery organizations, such as Camfed, an NGO that has supported the education of over 500,000 girls in the most deprived communities of Zimbabwe, Tanzania, Ghana, Zambia and Malawi; or iMlango, an NGO that establishes schools in rural areas of Kenya with an individualized e-learning platform, computer tablets and broadband access.

As with the Educate Girls project discussed earlier, the outcome fund model is being used to help it scale up. The British Asian Trust's outcome fund has raised $11 million to expand the project throughout Rajasthan, Gujarat and Delhi, which will help 200,000 children.[36]

One of the most promising efforts in development is being led by the government of Liberia. The Liberian Educational Advancement Program (LEAP) represents an early step towards introducing the approach of an outcome fund to social service delivery in the country. It aims to improve educational attainment in the country's schools – 25 per cent of 15–24-year-olds are illiterate, and 52 per cent of primary-school-age children were not enrolled in 2015.[37] While LEAP currently operates as a public–private partnership, the goal is for LEAP to become an outcome-based program, in which the achievement of targeted outcomes will dictate payments made to LEAP by outcome funders.[38]

> Philanthropy must ... catalyze systemic change, if we are to improve lives on a global scale

I believe that Outcome Funds will catalyze breakthroughs that will enable the world's best NGOs and social entrepreneurs to raise more money, scale their operations and help more people. The scale of our problems requires powerful new mechanisms. Large Outcome Funds will make it easier to get bigger SIBs and DIBs off the ground, reduce the time and cost it takes to launch them, and by multiplying and extending interventions, will bring systemic change in education, healthcare, employment and the environment, changing the reality on the ground and resulting in more effective programs.

In a world with ever greater problems, scaling up solutions is imperative. Sally Osberg and Roger Martin have stressed the importance of making systemic change if we really want to tackle social and environmental issues.[39]

As money flows into multi-billion-dollar Outcome Funds and they attract large SIB and DIB funds to invest opposite them, impact entrepreneurs leading delivery organizations will be able to raise the funding they need to implement their innovative approaches at scale, bringing systemic change – just as venture capital and tech entrepreneurs brought systemic change through the Tech Revolution.

Unleashing the Endowment

Of course, grant-making is only one part of the traditional philanthropic foundation's model. There's also the endowment of a foundation whose total investable assets are huge compared to grants. A typical foundation might invest about 95 per cent of its money in the investment market and give away 5 per cent each year in grants. The goal is to spend less in grants than the endowment's investments are making, so that the foundation can continue to exist and give away money. The Heron Foundation's Clara Miller has aptly described this traditional foundation model as 'a hedge fund with a small giving program welded onto the side'.

What does this model mean for philanthropists? Imagine you're the executive director of a charitable foundation and you're meeting with the foundation's investment advisors. You will talk about maximizing the return on the foundation's endowment, which this year might mean investing in some major polluters or maybe even a couple of fossil fuel companies. You'll also be meeting with one of your grantees, a fantastic non-profit that's working hard to help indigenous people in their fight to preserve their habitat, protect wildlife and fight climate change.

The irony might not be lost on you: your investments are helping to create the problems that you are trying to solve with your grants, but you feel obliged to maximize the returns on your investments. You wish you could be sure that you are having a net positive impact on the environment through your grants and endowment, but you do not know how to calculate that. At the same time, your grantees will report on their activity, rather than on their impact – on how many new spokespeople they have trained and how many protests they have organized rather than on how many tons of carbon dioxide are being captured by the land they are protecting. Without any way to measure the impact on either side of this equation, all you can do is hope that your grants do more to help the environment than your investments are doing to harm it.

This contradiction is not imaginary – it is the way philanthropy has operated for a century – and the problem is not confined to environmental charities. Foundations devoted to alleviating poverty invest in companies that pay poverty wages, and foundations devoted to refugee rights in conflict situations invest in arms companies.

There are good reasons for the double bind in which philanthropy finds itself. Firstly, regulations generally require directors and trustees of foundations to focus on generating investment returns and limit their ability to use their endowments' investment portfolios to advance their mission. The traditional model of foundations separates the endowment from their mission – by making as much money as possible, they can give away as much as possible. And as there is no commonly accepted way to measure the impact of different companies' activities on society and the environment, it is difficult to make the case for avoiding certain investments and for seeking others.

This contradiction has been acknowledged by the Ford Foundation's visionary CEO, Darren Walker: 'As a global foundation committed to fighting injustice, it is not lost on my colleagues and me that the very same systems that produce inequality also created our endowment, which, wisely invested, continues to fund our fight *against* inequality.'[40] Impact investment explodes that old irony and unleashes the power of endowments to help foundations achieve the maximum net positive impact. Through impact investment, the endowment of a foundation contributes to achieving its mission, rather than working against it.

Impact investing represents a totally different way of thinking about the purpose and practice of philanthropy, but it's far from a hostile takeover of philanthropy by private-sector investors.[41] Just as Darren Walker has, many people in the foundation and non-profit worlds have been searching for a better way for years. Impact investment offers innovative foundations a way to achieve greater impact with their money, while still achieving market rates of return.

Some foundations have been reluctant to move their endowments into impact investing because of a perceived obligation for trustees to maximize endowment returns, but as impact thinking spreads, some of these limitations are being redefined. For example, in the US, the Department of the Treasury issued new guidelines, in 2016, that were designed to promote impact investing. The director of the Office of Social Innovation and Civic Participation made the opportunity clear: 'A foundation manager can factor in how the anticipated charitable outcomes from the investment might further the foundation's mission in addition to the financial returns that are typically considered ... without fear of facing a tax penalty.'[42] Foundations are slowly beginning to take notice, with more of them using their endowments as another tool to achieve their missions.

In the UK too, a new Charities Act was passed in 2016 to make it clear that the obligation of foundation trustees is not just to make money, but to achieve a reasonable financial, social and environmental return. This act both defines 'social investments' and gives charities the power to make them. According to the act, 'A social investment is made when a relevant act of a charity is carried out with a view to both: (a) directly furthering the charity's purposes; and (b) achieving a financial return for the charity ... An incorporated charity has, and the charity trustees of an unincorporated charity have, power to make social investments.'[43]

These changes have encouraged foundations to enter the impact investing field, with far-reaching significance. For example, Guy's and St Thomas' Charity, an independent London-based health foundation, now invests at least 5 per cent of its endowment of nearly £800 million ($1.1 billion) to 'support better health' in society. In doing so, it has backed a specialist healthcare investor, Apposite Capital, which invests in businesses that deliver high-quality, affordable care.[44] The foundation has also used its £380 million ($505.4 million) property portfolio to host healthcare facilities[45] – its aim is to maximize its positive impact by channeling all its assets towards achieving its charitable mission.

The Ford Foundation, under the leadership of Darren Walker and its investment savvy chairman, Peter Nadosy, is leading the way in using the endowment to achieve a blend of financial, social and environmental returns. In April 2017, the foundation's board approved a $1 billion allocation to mission-related investment (MRI)[46] from its $12 billion endowment[47] – the largest endowment commitment to date.[48]

Interestingly, this is not the first time that the Ford Foundation has led innovation in philanthropy. In 1968, it introduced program-related investments (PRIs) – investments that qualify as grants because of their high philanthropic contribution and the high level of financial risk involved. To date, Ford has deployed more than $670 million in PRI to complement its grant-making across its program initiatives,[49] and it currently manages a $280 million PRI allocation.[50] PRI differs from MRI as it is treated as a grant and counts towards the 5 per cent of the endowment's value that must be given away annually to maintain the foundation's favorable tax status. In contrast, MRI is investment that seeks social and financial returns but is made from the undistributed 95 per cent of the foundation's endowment.

The Ford Foundation's mission-related investment program represents a supplementary 8 per cent of the endowment, which is used to achieve the foundation's mission. This allocation targets investments that can deliver market-rate financial returns, which are generally higher than the average return yielded by PRI investments. Together, the grant program and the endowment can combine to help achieve the foundation's philanthropic goals.

How has Ford spent its $1 billion endowment allocation? Well, for example, $30 million has gone towards MRIs tackling the affordable housing crisis in the USA – including investing in a community-improvement development bond from Capital Impact Partners and funding housing developers, such as Jonathan Rose and Avanath, that create affordable and green housing.[51] This approach makes so much sense, that Ford is now working towards doing the same but for financial services for the poor.[52]

As Darren Walker puts it, 'If the last fifty years of philanthropy were defined by grant-making budgets, the next fifty must be about directing the other 95 per cent of our assets toward justice.' Walker acknowledges that it will take a lot more than Ford's $1 billion allocation to solve our systemic social and environmental problems, and sees Ford's commitment as encouraging other foundations to get on board. And with US-based private foundations holding over $850 billion[53] in endowments,[54] and non-US foundations holding approximately $650 billion, the potential for foundations to deliver a significantly greater impact is huge.

Other US foundations are beginning to follow Ford's lead. The Kresge Foundation has set an objective to invest 10 per cent of its endowment, $350 million, in social investments by 2020. The David and Lucile Packard Foundation, which has a $6.9 billion endowment, has instituted a $180 million mandate for impact investment.[55] And in Canada, the J.W. McConnell Family Foundation is set to exceed its impact investment allocation of 10 per cent.[56]

In Portugal, the Calouste Gulbenkian Foundation is among those leading the way in Europe. Most recently it invested from its endowment in the €40 million ($ 44.4 million) MAZE Mustard Seed Social Entrepreneurship Fund, which aims to scale early-stage technology to solve meaningful global problems. The fund invests in start-ups tackling issues ranging from food waste to education and the social integration of migrants and refugees.[57]

Further afield, Japan's Sasakawa Peace Foundation (SPF) is moving in the same direction. Mari Kogiso, director of the Gender Investment and Innovation Department at SPF, has said that 'grant-making is not always the most effective tool' for SPF to meet its objectives, which is why it began exploring impact investing.[58] Stepping in this direction, the foundation launched the Asian Women's Impact Fund in 2017, a $100 million fund that promotes women's empowerment and gender equality. In 2018, the fund invested one billion yen

($9.5 million) in BlueOrchard's Microfinance Fund in support of women's empowerment.[59]

Going further still, a number of family foundations are now dedicating 100 per cent of their endowments to impact investment. Notable among these are the Heron Foundation, whose endowment is $300 million.[60] The foundation regards ensuring that 100 per cent of its assets are invested in line with Heron's mission as its fiduciary duty.[61]

Heron have changed their foundation's operational structure to reflect this new way of working. Instead of having an investing side that focuses on maximizing financial returns for the endowment and a separate giving side which donates 5 per cent of the endowment each year, they have merged the two together. This contrasts with the old set-up which Miller describes as 'a black and white universe'.[62] Now 'everyone works to maximize social and financial missions together to be a positive force,' says Miller.

The Nathan Cummings Foundation has followed the example of the Heron Foundation and allocated its entire $500 million endowment to ESG and impact investment.[63] The former president and CEO Sharon Alpert recognizes the power of using the endowment and encourages others to utilize it: 'Foundations have trillions in assets, but often don't recognize or activate the full extent of their resources. By harnessing the full potential of our assets ... we can activate the power of our investments to achieve the future we all want and deserve.'[64]

Silicon Valley alumni Charly and Lisa Kleissner's KL Felicitas Foundation is going all-in by dedicating its total assets of approximately $10 million to impact investing,[65] and they are encouraging their peers to do the same. Under the umbrella of Toniic, a global action community of impact investors, the Kleissners co-founded the '100 per cent Impact Network', a collaborative group of more than one hundred family offices, high-net worth individuals and foundations (23 per cent are family foundations, according to their 2018 report)[66] who have each pledged to dedicate their portfolios to impact investment. The group has a collective $6 billion of assets, with more than $3 billion already deployed,[67] and aims to create an international movement of impact investors.[68]

The New Kids on the Block

A new crop of foundations, led by individuals who have achieved great success in business and technology, are the primary drivers of a new philanthropic model. They focus on sustainable, long-term funding rather than short-term grant-giving, and increasingly look at the outcomes rather than the activities of service providers, encouraging innovation and striving to make the best use of their philanthropic resources, with the aim of creating the biggest positive impact.

Who better to bring capitalism's best tools into philanthropy than some of the world's most successful entrepreneurs-turned-philanthropists? The Omidyar Network, launched by eBay founder Pierre Omidyar and his wife Pamela, is a big player among the new generation of philanthropists who are changing how the sector acts. The organization is a hybrid model, made up of a foundation and an impact investing firm. They make grants and PRIs through the former and invest in purpose-driven businesses through the latter. But this was not how they started.

It was Pierre Omidyar's frustration with traditional philanthropy and its limitations, alongside his experience of the power of business to create impact at scale, that led him to this model: 'We created a foundation and after a few years of trying to do traditional philanthropy, just simple grant-making, I became a little bit frustrated because at the same time I was seeing the social impact eBay was having as a private business. It was improving people's lives by creating a platform where people could meet each other around shared interests; people were creating businesses, employment was being created, lives were being improved and I saw the potential that business could have to make the world better. So, in 2003–04, we said, 'OK, that's enough of the ... purely foundation approach,' and we reorganized ourselves into the Omidyar Network.'[69]

Referring to themselves as a 'philanthropic investment firm', the Omidyar Network engages in both traditional grant-making and investing, bringing philanthropy and the private sector 'together around the same mission of trying to create opportunity for people around the world'.[70] Refugees United, a web-based platform that helps to reunite displaced people with missing family members, is one of their non-profit grantees, while d.light, which provides affordable solar-powered lights for poor communities in Africa, is one of their for-profit investees.[71] Both sides are working in harmony towards the foundation's mission.

So far, around half of Omidyar's $1.5 billion total commitment has gone to non-profit grants, and half has gone to profit-with-purpose investments.[72] As well as putting all of its philanthropic dollars towards impact, Omidyar also believes in embracing risk, which is why the Omidyar Network dedicates 10 per cent of all its spending to experiments and learning. Omidyar says that philanthropists 'ought to be in a position of taking on more risk than they traditionally do'. Citing the venture capital sector, he says, 'these guys are at the pinnacle of all of the forces that have led to the creation of talent' and that philanthropists should learn from them.[73]

The Omidyar Network has also been one of the largest supporters of the impact investing sector. Its former CEO, Matt Bannick, represented the US on the G8 Social Impact Investment Taskforce and greatly supported the effort of its US National Advisory Board, as well as Social Finance US, the GSG and the Education Outcomes Fund for Africa and the Middle East. His successor, Mike Kubzansky, is very committed to efforts to reimagine capitalism. Together with the Skoll Foundation, which was set up in 1999 by Jeff Skoll, the former CEO of eBay, Omidyar has been the most prominent figure to support the growth of impact investment.

In a similar way to the Omidyar Network, the Skoll Foundation aims to achieve systemic change on a global scale through the power of innovation and entrepreneurship – hallmarks of the new model of impact philanthropy. As well as believing that 'social entrepreneurs are the world's best bet for solving some of the world's thorniest problems', Jeff Skoll promotes long-term funding to support these entrepreneurs, in order to 'help them scale their innovations', since 'unrestricted funding plays an important role in innovation and entrepreneurial growth'.[74]

Skoll allocates its grant and PRI money within an explicit outcome framework. In addition, its endowment is invested for impact through Skoll's investment management firm, Capricorn Investment Group – a certified B Corp.[75]

Keen that both its grant and its investment dollars should make a difference, it was the Skoll Foundation that originally pushed Capricorn towards utilizing impact investing as a way of aligning its investments with the foundation's mission. As Capricorn managing principal Ion Yadigaroglu and managing director Alan Chang explain, 'Early on, when the foundation would ask about our investing, we'd say, "Our job is to invest money, your job is to give it away." But the foundation wasn't satisfied with this conventional answer, and they pushed us to think more about the positive and negative impacts of our investments.'[76]

Since then, Capricorn has invested in Tesla and other carbon-reducing enterprises including QuantumScape, a technology company that's developing lithium batteries, Joby Aviation, which is creating electric-powered air taxis, and Saildrone, which designs wind-powered oceangoing drones for autonomous data collection.[77]

The Bill and Melinda Gates Foundation, the largest foundation in the world, with an endowment of about $45 billion, has brought business methods to philanthropy and takes an outcome-oriented approach to grant-making. Instead of asking grantees to report on their activities, they look for ways to measure results.[78]

Gates doesn't just make grants. Through its Strategic Investment Fund (SIF), set up in 2009, it also makes low-interest loans, equity investments and provides volume guarantees for for-profit companies that are taking aim at big problems.[79] It uses these tools to leverage the power of private-sector innovation, using different approaches to tackle different problems at scale.

For example, to help women around the world gain access to affordable contraception, the foundation guaranteed $120 million in sales of contraceptive implants – one of the most effective and user-friendly forms of birth control on the market. The guarantee ensured a viable market for manufacturers Bayer and Merck & Co, and in exchange the manufacturers agreed to lower the price of the implants.[80] Thanks to this effort, more than 42 million of them have been distributed in some of the world's poorest countries.[81]

When it comes to equity investments, Gates targets early-stage biotech companies. As an early-stage investor, it has the power to influence investee companies. In this way, it can ensure that scientific and technological advances are applied to diseases affecting the world's poorest populations. This includes ensuring that the products and tools developed by investee companies are affordable to these poorest populations. So far the foundation has made around 40 such investments totaling $700 million,[82] including in CureVac, which develops vaccines against cancer and infectious disease, Vir Biotechnology, which develops immune programming technology, and Intarcia Therapeutics, which is working to transform the management of chronic diseases like diabetes and HIV through new drug delivery technology.[83]

One of the most promising new family foundations is the Chan Zuckerberg Initiative (CZI). In 2015, at the age of 30, Mark Zuckerberg and his wife Priscilla Chan announced that they plan to direct 99 per cent of their $45 billion[84] wealth into CZI. Their goal is to make a substantial commitment to impact investing that is focused on 'personalized, learning, curing disease, connecting people and building strong communities'.[85]

Chan and Zuckerberg take an unconventional approach to philanthropy. They set up CZI as a Limited Liability Corporation (LLC), rather than a traditional foundation, which means they're not limited by the regulations that foundations have to abide by. CZI can make money by investing in impact initiatives and re-invest that money into other impact organizations. Newer foundations like this one are often more willing to experiment with outcome funding and pay-for-success approaches than more established ones are.

These 'new kids on the block' are being joined by some long-established foundations, which are experimenting with new philanthropic models. For example, the MacArthur Foundation is leading a new effort to scale the funding of charitable organizations by attracting impact investment through what it calls 'catalytic capital'. This means providing funding from its grant money at concessionary terms in order to attract outside capital from investors. MacArthur has recently teamed up with the Rockefeller Foundation and the Omidyar Network to provide $150 million of cheap debt and equity, through the Catalytic Capital Consortium. Its aim is to help charitable organizations become impact investment-ready and help them to scale by attracting significant investment money.[86] It is likely that a combination of long-established philanthropists like these and new kids on the block will together lead the advance of impact philanthropy.

A Moment of Reckoning

At a session at the 2019 Skoll World Forum in Oxford, the audience was asked whether it felt that philanthropy was at a moment of reckoning. Nearly everyone present agreed that it was.[87] Impact philanthropy is crystalizing that moment of reckoning by affirming that we must focus on outcomes over activities, that we can measure outcomes, that we should use pay-for-outcomes in grant-making, and that a foundation's endowment should help achieve its philanthropic mission.

The nature of foundations makes them a perfect leader of the Impact Revolution. Because of their charitable status and sense of mission, they can experiment with different roles – acting as grantors, investors, guarantors or outcome payers. They can fund efforts to support the growth of the impact field, as well as influence delivery organizations, governments and investors to collaborate in new ways in tackling social problems.

They also have an important role to play in funding the advance of the impact movement itself. All big movements, including recent neoliberalism, were funded by philanthropists, and the same is becoming true of the impact movement. The

Omidyar Network, Ford, Rockefeller, MacArthur, Kresge and Hewlett Foundation in the US; Europe's Bertelsmann Stiftung[88] in Germany and the Calouste Gulbenkian Foundation[89] in Portugal; Lord (Jacob) Rothschild's family foundation, Yad Hanadiv, and the Edmond de Rothschild Foundation, in Israel; and Ratan Tata and the Tata Trusts, in India, have all supported the impact movement.

Given that philanthropy has an obligation to deploy its resources in the most effective way in order to help the greatest number of people, it must grasp the opportunity that impact investment offers. Foundations must take risks, fund innovation and use both grants and endowments to pursue their mission. Impact investment and its new tools, SIBs, DIBs and Outcome Funds, equip philanthropy to tackle our biggest problems. As the natural torchbearer of the impact movement, philanthropy has the power to usher in a new dawn for charitable organizations, investors, entrepreneurs, businesses and governments, to bring solutions to the greatest social and environmental problems of our time.

Chapter 6

GOVERNMENT: SOLVING BIGGER PROBLEMS, FASTER

We must shift our economies to create positive outcomes

Our economic system is self-defeating. Unfettered, capitalism creates huge social and environmental problems, which governments try to fix by taxing everyone, while investors and companies focus only on making money. It makes no sense.

Impact changes everything. It transforms the private sector from a polluter and a driver of inequality into a powerful force for good. By working to optimize risk–return–impact, entrepreneurs and companies create new products and services that improve lives and our planet. And given the scale of the social and environmental challenges facing us today, governments need businesses to play a central role in developing new solutions. It is the way we will transition to impact economies, where decisions regarding consumption and investment are based on risk–return–impact.

Transitioning to a true impact economy will represent a fundamental change in how our economies work – a shift from seeing business and investment as purely about profit to understanding that they are necessary to bring about the solutions we need. Both the private sector and governments need to do their part: the private sector must innovate and create new solutions, and governments need to embrace new ways of tackling big problems.

> Impact changes everything. It transforms the private sector from a polluter and a driver of inequality into a powerful force for good

How Impact Investment Can Help Governments Do Their Job

Governments have huge power to initiate change and direct progress. They realize that economic growth has not provided the solutions we hoped for – that our communities need more than just an increase in the average standard of living. Those who have been left behind by growing prosperity are most often unable to escape their difficult circumstances, which they sometimes find themselves in from birth. If you are born into a family with unemployed parents who have a drug habit, there is a high chance that you will end up trapped in the same cycle.

Poverty, under-education, unemployment, an aging pop-ulation and environmental destruction are just some of the challenges confronting us. Despite trying hard, governments have failed to find the needed solutions. I believe part of the reason is that they are not naturally suited for risky invest-ment, innovation and the occasional failure. So what do we do? That's where impact investment comes in.

Previous chapters have shown how impact positively disrupts the prevailing models of entrepreneurship, invest-ment, big business and philanthropy. It also brings several transformational forces to help governments solve bigger problems, faster:

One: It brings the measurement of social outcomes achieved by government spending, making government more transparent, accountable and effective.

Two: It harnesses private capital and entrepreneurship, in much the same way as the Tech Revolution did, to stimulate innovation in tackling social and environmental issues. In so doing it unites investors, charitable organizations, businesses, philanthropists and governments in the drive to solve big problems.

Three: It introduces pay-for-outcomes approaches to public service procurement and attracts philanthropists to contribute through Outcome Funds, and private investors to provide the upfront money needed through SIB and DIB funds. This ensures that government money is spent effectively, because government only pays for outcomes that have been achieved.

Four: It can access money that is public money but not tax money, such as unclaimed assets in banks, insurance companies and investment funds. This money can be used to develop a strong sector of impact investment managers who provide start-up and growth capital to charitable organizations and purpose-driven businesses.

Shifting the mindset of government procurement from prescribing services in detail to paying for outcomes achieved through SIBs will drive the use of pay-for-outcomes approaches, and create a thriving outcomes market for the first time. Our best chance of finding urgent solutions is for governments to encourage the development of impact investment in all its forms, pay-for-outcomes models and impact measurement by companies and investors.

In this way, governments can accelerate the transition to risk–return–impact economies. They are best positioned to catalyze rapid growth in impact investment, just as they did for venture capital in the late 1970s.

In the US, back in 1979, an amendment to the Employee Retirement Income Security Act (ERISA) resulted in a dramatic increase in the supply of available capital, as company pension funds were allowed to invest in venture funds.[1] Before this, they had been severely limited in how much they could allocate to high-risk assets, including venture capital. After 1979, pension fund commitments to venture capital rose dramatically as a result, from $100–200 million a year during the 1970s, to more than $4 billion each year by the end of the 1980s.[2] This important change in regulation combined with the reduction of capital gains tax to 28 per cent in 1978 and to 20 per cent in 1981 gave a big boost to venture capital, which has since grown to become about a trillion-dollar global pool.

The role of governments in creating systemic change is crucial. Mariana Mazzucato rightly argues in *The Entrepreneurial State* that governments have actively shaped and created markets. This is what governments need to do for the impact market today. They can stimulate its growth in very clear ways – here is how.

Nine Things For Governments To Do

As a report by The Global Steering Group for Impact Investment (GSG)[3] has shown, various governments across the world – including the UK, the US, France, Japan, Canada, Italy, South Korea, Israel, Portugal and Australia – have already begun implementing initiatives to stimulate the flow of impact investment in their countries. If all nine of the following measures are adopted widely, it would fundamentally change the world.

1. Require companies to measure their impact

The financial crisis of 2008, which has been widely attributed to the self-interested excesses of bankers, led to widespread discontent with our whole financial system; in many ways, it opened the door to today's raging debate about the need to overhaul our system, much like the Wall Street Crash did in

1929. If impact economies are the answer to the challenges of the twenty-first century, and standardized impact measurement is essential to creating them, governments should take the lead in requiring companies *now* to collect and audit impact data on their activities.

Many governments have already started on the way to doing that. For instance, Japan established its Social Impact Measurement Initiative (SIMI) in 2016. With over 130 members, including funds, companies, non-profits and intermediaries, this initiative provides guidance on universal impact measurement. France has developed its own tool to measure and monitor social impact, MESIS, through NovESS, the government-sponsored investment fund for impact businesses. In Italy, the Ministry of Education, Research and Universities has supported ten Italian universities that are developing new knowledge on impact measurement.

EU member states have also had to integrate the Non-Financial Reporting Directive of 2014 into their own national legislation.[4] This requires companies with over 500 employees to publish a non-financial information statement (NFIS), which provides a comprehensive picture of a company's social and environmental impact. These regulations provide a good base for the adoption of impact-weighted financial accounts, and are a good first step towards the creation of an EU-wide impact economy.

More recently, at the end of 2019, the EU issued new disclosure regulation that requires investors to publish the procedures they use to integrate ESG risks into their investment and advisory processes. The aim is to enable informed choices that would lead to a more responsible financial system.[5]

When governments require all businesses and investors to measure and report on their impact, this will mark the beginning of a new era, in which our norms around 'value' and 'success' align with society's needs.

2. Appoint a cabinet-level minister to lead impact policy

Establishing a dedicated government department led by a minister for impact is essential to ensuring that impact is established as an active government priority. Such a minister is responsible for creating a national impact strategy, developing supportive policies and fostering cooperation on impact initiatives among all government departments.

In 2003, Tony Blair's Labour government in the UK set up a central unit to support what was then known as the 'social investment sector'. After David Cameron's Conservative election win in 2010, he elevated responsibility for impact investment to the Cabinet Office which reports directly to the prime minister, where Francis Maude, Nick Hurd and Kieron Boyle led, among many other initiatives, the effort to establish Big Society Capital as a social investment bank that can drive the advance of the impact ecosystem; a year later, in 2013, the same Cabinet Office supported the creation of and provided the secretariat for the G8 Social Impact Investment Task Force. Today, this unit continues its work within the Office for Civil Society.

The governments of Brazil, France, Canada, Portugal and South Korea have all set up dedicated government units. In Brazil, the office is the Secretariat for Innovation and New Business and is part of the Ministry of Industry.[6] It has developed ENIMPACTO, a ten-year strategy for impact investing that has been helpful in boosting Brazil's impact sector.

In France, the Ministry for Ecological and Inclusive Transition has recently become an active driver of impact investment through legislation, regulation and the media. It has also promoted an international agenda for creating, promoting and strengthening impact economies, through an alliance it has called Pact for Impact.

3. Publish the cost of social issues

Calculating the cost of social issues for the government is a crucial first step in the development of outcome-based approaches – it is essential for quantifying and monetizing social impact and also for tying social impact to financial return. After all, if you don't know the cost of recidivism, how can you work out a fair price for reducing it? Making this information publicly available helps to create the foundations for an outcome-based investment market.

With this in mind, the UK's Cabinet Office published the Unit Cost Database in 2014 to provide estimates for more than 600 social costs, including education and skills, employment, health, crime, housing and social services.[7] The most comprehensive attempt to date to quantify such costs, it has become an integral part of the UK's impact investment ecosystem.

So far, Portugal is the only other country to have followed suit, setting up its own government cost database in 2017. An online portal provides more than 90 social cost indicators[8] – for example, it shows that it costs €42 ($47) per day to keep an offender in prison and €137 ($145) per day to house a young offender in a juvenile detention center.[9]

Some non-governmental initiatives are going in the same direction as these cost databases: the UK's Global Value Exchange, set up by the non-profit Social Value UK – a long-standing proponent of impact measurement, is a free online platform that offers a crowd-sourced database of values, outcomes, indicators and stakeholders, comprising over 30,000 global impact measurement metrics.[10]

4. Shift government focus from inputs to outcomes

When it comes to tackling the social and environmental problems we face today, there is no time – or money – to waste, which is why it is so important that governments shift their focus from inputs to outcomes. As we have already seen, focusing on outcomes is the best way to identify the most efficient interventions and implement them at scale. Many more governments should choose to focus on outcomes, and the launch of SIBs is most often the best place for them to start doing so.

> When it comes to tackling the social and environmental problems we face today, there is no time – or money – to waste

The French government began launching social impact bonds, or 'social impact contracts' as they are known there, in 2016. There are currently six confirmed French SIBs. The first, led by Adie, issues microloans to people with no access to the job market or the banking system who want to start a business. The second, led by Passeport Avenir, helps people from disadvantaged backgrounds continue their education by offering them financial support, up to postgraduate level.[11] Private sector leaders are following the government's lead, with BNP Paribas, the country's largest bank, investing in all of these French SIBs.

Finland has seven outcome-based projects that are either active or in development. It has launched the largest SIB in Europe, a €14.2 million ($15.8 million) impact bond that supports refugee and immigrant integration, and is preparing to launch the first European environmental impact bond.

Through the leadership of Yaron Neudorfer, CEO of Social Finance Israel, the Israeli government has participated directly and indirectly in two SIBs: one aimed at preventing type2 diabetes and the other at improving educational attainment in mathematics among Bedouin youth.[12]

The Portland Trust, the non-profit 'action tank' which I co-founded with Sir Harry Solomon in 2003 to work on the economic dimension of peace between Israelis and Palestinians, put together another diabetes prevention DIB in Palestine in 2017. The Bank of Palestine provided the investment money and the Palestine Telecommunications Company was the principal outcome payer, alongside the Palestinian Authority. This small DIB was followed by a $5 million World Bank Palestinian Employment DIB in 2019, in which the World Bank is the outcome payer through the Palestinian Ministry of Finance, and the investors include the Palestine Investment Fund, Invest Palestine, the European Bank for Reconstruction and Development and FMO, the Dutch development finance institution.

In Argentina, the first government-backed SIB was launched in Buenos Aires in 2018. This impact bond, which targets employment for vulnerable youths in the south of the city, is funded by institutional and private investors and viewed by the government as a pilot for future SIBs in the region.[13]

The UK government was the first to launch a dedicated fund to experiment with SIBs. In 2012, the Department for Work and Pensions launched a £30 million ($39.9 million) innovation fund to pay for the outcomes of SIBs directed at helping disadvantaged young people. At the same time, the UK government raised the profile of impact within procurement through the Social Value Act in 2012, which requires public sector commissioning to consider economic, social and environmental factors, in addition to price, in the tendering process.[14]

Now the UK has embarked on the next logical step, which is to assign a bigger chunk of commissioning to outcome-based programs. The UK government is using outcome-based contracting in the areas of employment, healthcare, prisoner reintegration and international development. One example is its Troubled Families program, which has allocated over £1 billion ($1.33 billion) to help over 500,000 vulnerable families deal with truancy, unemployment, mental health problems, domestic abuse and crime.[15]

In addition to making government spending more effective, greater outcome-based commissioning helps to create a flourishing SIB market, attracting private capital to support governments' efforts.

5. Create central Outcome Funds to boost effective service delivery

Central Outcome Funds catalyze outcome-based contracts, including SIBs and DIBs. When run at scale, they have the influence to stimulate cooperation between government, philanthropists and the private sector, as well as the design of programs that support government policy. They also generate evidence that shows what works, how much it costs and the subsequent savings to government.

Evidence from the Bridges SIB funds in the UK, which we discussed earlier, shows that £46 million ($61.2 million) of outcome payments created nearly £80 million ($106.4 million) in value for the government departments that paid for them, not taking into account substantial long-term savings in health, welfare, justice and other services.[16]

The UK launched the first central Outcome Fund in 2016: the £80 million ($106.4 million) Life Chances Fund (LCF) is designed to help those who face the most significant challenges, focusing on drug and alcohol dependency, children's services, young people and the elderly. The fund contributes around 20 per cent of total outcome payments with local commissioners paying the remaining cost, an approach that recognizes that outcomes and savings fall on local as well as central government. The LCF expects to leverage a further £320 million ($425.6 million) from local commissioners, creating a pool of £400 million for outcome contracts.

In the US, the Social Impact Partnerships to Pay for Results Act (SIPPRA), passed by Congress in 2018, provides a $92 million fund for outcome-based financing at the Department of Treasury. Targeted outcomes include improved child and maternal health, reduced homelessness, lowered rates of recidivism and increased youth employment, with the main requirement being that outcomes must 'result in social benefit and Federal, State or local savings'.

6. Integrate impact investment into international development aid

As mentioned previously, achieving the UN's Social Development Goals will require $3.3–$4.5 trillion each year over the next decade. Global development flows account for roughly $1.4 trillion per year, (including foreign direct investment, debt and equity flows, official aid and investment by development finance institutions), which leaves an annual shortfall of about $2.5 trillion.[17] Since government budget constraints are increasingly tight and there is public pressure to demonstrate effective public spending, international development cannot rely only on its traditional tools –it needs to find new ways to tackle development challenges.

Governments recognize the need for new approaches: at their 2019 meeting, the development ministers of countries in the G7 announced their support for impact investment, the development of impact bonds and Outcome Funds, and 'the growth of the impact investing market as a meaningful and efficient financing force which can contribute to the 2030 Agenda'. They also acknowledged the need for governments to create 'enabling policy environments', in support of impact investing in the developing world.[18]

Official development agencies, including the Department for International Development in the UK (DFID) and the Agency for International Development in the US (USAID), are already starting to integrate impact measurement and investment into their activities. DFID launched its Impact Programme in 2012 and planned to provide up to £160 million ($212.8 million) over 23 years, in order to catalyze the market for impact investment in sub-Saharan Africa and South Asia.[19] The program invests through CDC, the UK's development finance institution (DFI) that acts as the investment arm of DFID. CDC has a portfolio of $5.5 billion in equity and debt investments in Africa and South Asia, and has recently allocated $1.5 billion to a new Catalyst Strategies initiative, to 'shape nascent markets and build more inclusive and sustainable economies', by taking 'a flexible approach to risk in exchange for pioneering impact'.[20]

With their huge resources, DFIs like CDC in the UK and OPIC in the US are powerful investors in emerging markets. It is, therefore, very significant that they are now getting involved in driving the growth of impact investment, measurement and pay-for-outcomes programs.

Government development agencies can boost their impact by establishing Outcome Funds, while their DFIs can invest in DIBs. An interesting example of this new model at work is the $5.28 million Village Enterprise DIB, which aims to transform the lives of more than 12,000 households in rural Kenya and Uganda by creating more than 4,000 sustainable microenterprises over four years.[21] The first DIB in the world to focus specifically on poverty alleviation and the first to target sub-Saharan Africa, it has attracted aid contributions from USAID and DFID to pay for the outcomes it achieves.[22]

In this particular case, USAID, DFID and other donors make contributions to an Outcome Fund that is managed by a third party. If Village Enterprise delivers its goals in reducing poverty, the original investors will be paid back through the outcome fund. Village Enterprise benefits because it raises more capital than it could have raised through traditional grants,[23] while USAID and DFID only pay for the outcomes Village Enterprise actually achieve.

7. Release unclaimed assets to establish 'impact capital wholesalers'

Imagine that you could snap your fingers and create an extra $2.5 billion in a country's budget, without either raising taxes or cutting crucial programs. Governments around the world are starting to discover that they can do this by using unclaimed assets, essentially creating money out of thin air.

Unclaimed assets, which means bank accounts, insurance policies and investments that have been separated from their owners for many years, represent a compelling source of public money for governments to use in tackling social issues. Indeed, a few governments are already using this 'free money' to accelerate the growth of impact investing by creating impact capital wholesalers.

Impact capital wholesalers provide funding for impact investment firms, encourage other investors to chip in, promote the measurement of impact and develop the impact ecosystem through education and collaboration. They can invest both in the impact investment firms themselves or in the funds that these firms manage. They can also act as champions of the impact sector, popularizing it and encouraging government policy to support it. They can be funded through the release of unclaimed assets, directly by government, by the private sector, or by all three.

The UK was the first country that saw the potential of unclaimed assets to spark real change in society. In 2011, following the recommendation of the Commission on Unclaimed Assets (2005–7), which I chaired, Francis Maude, who was then leading the Cabinet Office, asked me and Nick O'Donohoe from JP Morgan to establish a social investment bank along the lines recommended by the Social Investment Task Force in 2000. The Cameron government, he informed me, was prepared to provide £400 million ($532 million) of unclaimed bank assets for this purpose.

In 2012, this money, having been supplemented by an additional £200 million ($266 million) from Barclays, HSBC, Lloyds and the Royal Bank of Scotland, went to establish Big Society Capital (BSC), with me as Chair and Nick O'Donohoe as CEO. Since then, an additional £600 million ($798 million) has been released to the Reclaim Fund,[24] which collects the the flow of unclaimed assets and distributes them according to the instruction of the government.

The role of BSC is to provide funding to investment managers who finance charities and social enterprises. Its objective is to build the infrastructure of a thriving impact sector that brings investment to social organizations that have previously depended exclusively on gifts and grants. It also drives the popularization of impact investment and represents the impact sector in policy discussion with government about social issues.

Since it was established, BSC has been responsible for investing, directly and with the co-investors it has attracted, £1.7 billion ($2.3 billion), which has funded more than 40 impact investment managers. These managers are using the funding to address a variety of social issues, including homelessness, affordable housing, youth unemployment, community organizations, childhood obesity and mental health.[25]

What does this achieve? In the words of BSC chairman Sir Harvey McGrath and former CEO Cliff Prior, it amounts to 'fueling powerful change – providing more than 1,100 innovative, hardworking and passionate social enterprises and charities with capital to improve the lives of people across the UK'.

Plans to expand the UK's flow of unclaimed assets, (which are also referred to as dormant assets), are under way: in 2019, the Dormant Assets Commission chaired by Nick O'Donohoe reported that up to an additional £2 billion ($2.7 billion) could be released from unclaimed assets held by insurance companies, pension funds and investment funds.

Several countries have followed the example of the UK in setting up impact wholesalers, sometimes by using unclaimed assets. Japan has announced the release of $3.5 billion in unclaimed bank assets to tackle social issues over the next five years. Its parliament passed the Dormant Account Utilization Bill in 2016 to channel funds from bank accounts that have been dormant for more than ten years into a new fund, the Designated Utilization Foundation.[26]

According to the GSG Japan National Advisory Board, it could result in up to $700 million a year for five years flowing to the private sector in the form of grants, loans and other funding.[27]

In other parts of the world, Portugal has established Portugal Inovação Social (PIS), a wholesaler funded with €150 million ($167 million) from the EU.[28] South Korea has announced a wholesaler funded with $300 million, half of which will come from the government and the other half from the private sector. Italy has allocated €25 million ($28 million) to Casa de Depositi e Prestiti (CDP), a financial service provider that has been charged with setting up an impact wholesaler. In 2019, Ireland introduced the Dormant Accounts Action Plan to provide over €30 million ($33.3 million) of funding in support of disadvantaged groups.[29] In Canada, the MaRS Center for Impact Investing has proposed using the $1 billion in unclaimed assets, (including unclaimed bank accounts, securities and court awards), for 'impact investments in affordable housing, employment, poverty reduction and other priority areas'.[30]

While it has not set up a new impact wholesaler as such, the US government has acted to supply impact capital through the Small Business Administration, which established a $1 billion fund for impact investing in 2011. This impact fund makes $200 million available each year to private equity funds to invest in small businesses that maximize financial return while also yielding measurable social, environmental or economic impact.[31]

My seven year experience at Big Society Capital has shown me how essential impact wholesalers are to the development of the impact investment market. Just as the stock market wouldn't work without intermediaries, the impact market also needs middlemen, in this case impact investment firms – which can be funded by impact wholesalers. While these impact investment firms may not yet seem as glamorous as venture capitalists or as iconic as the traders shouting on trading floors, like any market, the impact market cannot function or grow without them.

8. Boost the supply of impact capital through changes in regulation and tax incentives

The greatest levers at governments' disposal are those that affect the flow of capital from investors. As we have seen, asset management firms are involved in managing $85 trillion across the world, while pension funds manage $38 trillion.[32] These are colossal sums and if they are guided to achieve impact, they will significantly help government efforts to tackle the great social and environmental challenges we face. The explosion in venture capital in the 1980s offers an example of how an industry can be radically transformed through regulatory changes and tax incentives.

The UK is the first country to have introduced a specific incentive for 'social investment' in charitable organizations. The Social Investment Tax Relief (SITR) scheme was introduced in 2014 to provide 30 per cent tax relief for social investments. Investees who have benefited from the scheme include the Freedom Bakery in Glasgow, which trains prisoners to make artisan bread; FC United of Manchester, a co-operative that engages in youth work and adult education; and the heritage site Clevedon Pier near Bristol, which was renovated and restored with money raised through SITR.[33]

Unfortunately, EU 'state aid' regulations imposed a low ceiling on the amount per investor that can be invested through SITR, resulting in very little money flowing. A review of the scheme's rules is currently under way and I hope the ceiling will be raised significantly.

In the US, tax credits such as those that encourage developers to create affordable housing in low to moderate-income communities, have been a long-standing feature of social investment. More recent initiatives offer a reduction, deferral or elimination of capital gains tax liabilities on investments into designated Opportunity Zones.[34]

In France, a tax relief of 18 per cent on income and 50 per cent on estate tax[35] is offered to investors in solidarity funds and impact businesses; Portugal is one of the few countries to offer SIB incentives; Italy provides tax relief of 20–25 per cent for equity investments in small social enterprises; Argentina offers tax incentives for investments in renewable energy and in green bonds.[36]

In addition to tax incentives, supportive legislation and regulation can empower groups of investors, like pension funds and philanthropic endowments, to make impact investments. France is a leader in the pension fund area: its '90/10 legislation' was introduced in 2001 and then extended to all employee pension saving schemes throughout the country in 2008. Every third-party manager of pension savings schemes is now obligated to offer a 90/10 scheme, which allocates up to 10 per cent of its assets to unlisted social enterprises. The remaining 90 per cent are invested in listed companies, following socially responsible investment principles. As we have seen in Chapter 3, the increasing popularity of these funds has contributed to the growth of the market from €1 billion ($1.1 billion) in 2009 to approximately €10 billion ($11.1 billion) today, invested on behalf of more than one million members.[37]

Pension fund regulations are a priority for governments, given that pension funds hold so much money globally. It is reasonable for pension savers to be given the option, as happens in France, to choose savings programs that will invest in line with their values – for example, portfolios that aim to contribute to the achievement of the UN's Sustainable Development Goals.

More work remains to be done; the current regulatory framework, which imposes the pure pursuit of profit on most institutional investors, greatly inhibits the flow of capital into impact projects. The experience of my own firm, Apax Partners, shows what is possible when a change in regulations opens up a market. Our first fund in Europe, which was raised in 1981 to invest in the UK, amounted to just £10 million ($13.3 million).[38] Our last European fund before I left the firm, raised in 2002, amounted to €5 billion ($5.6 billion),[39] and Apax has since raised an €11 billion fund ($12.2 billion).

This is how financial markets work: new products take time to establish themselves, but once they are established, they grow exponentially. The growth of Apax benefited from changes in the regulatory environment surrounding pension funds, the establishment of incentives for entrepreneurs, and government support for entrepreneurs and venture capital. The same kind of support for impact investment today would create an even greater flow of capital.

9. Boost the demand for impact investment from charitable organizations and purpose-driven businesses

Governments can grow the supply of impact investment through regulatory changes, but they can also boost demand for it by supporting the development of charitable service providers and purpose-driven businesses – after all, the flood of capital we're hoping to unleash will need somewhere to go! Governments can provide financial support for incubators and accelerators that nurture purpose-driven enterprises, help prepare them for impact investment and mentor them so that they are capable of delivering impact at scale.

This is why the UK government established the Access Foundation in 2015, with co-investment from Big Society Capital and the Big Lottery Fund. This £100 million ($133 million) foundation aims to help early-stage social enterprises and charities access the finance they need to grow. It delivers support via two main programs: a growth fund that provides matched loan and grant capital of up to £150,000 ($200,000) per organization, and capacity-building programs to make impact organizations 'investment-ready'.[40]

The French government is working to support purpose-driven businesses: in 2016 it launched NovESS, a €100 million ($111 million) investment fund for impact businesses that's funded by public and private capital. A national accelerator for social innovation, Pioneers French Impact, is due to receive €1 billion ($1.1 billion) of funds over the next five years, which will support purpose-driven businesses on their journey to scale.

In Asia, South Korea has introduced new policy initiatives including the Korea Inclusive Finance Agency, a public financial institution that guarantees loans for businesses addressing social issues. The Korea Small and Medium Business Corporation (SBC) has been offering similar loan guarantees since the beginning of 2018.[41] Additionally, the Korea Social Enterprise Promotion Agency (KoSEA) is a government organization that runs acceleration and incubation programs for social enterprises.[42]

The Australian government has also taken steps to catalyze the impact investment market, although most of its initiatives have been limited in their scale. The Social Enterprise Development and Investment Funds program was established in 2011 through the country's Department of Education, Employment and Workplace Relations (DEEWR).[43] Initial grant funding of AU$20 million ($11.63 million) was matched by AU$20 million ($11.63 million) of private investment to help them expand.[44]

In Argentina, Fondece, a venture capital fund established by the Ministry of Production and Labor in 2017, will invest $172 million in VC funds and incubators working with impact businesses over four years. The Ministry of Environment has also set up PROESUS, a national program to support entrepreneurs, and specifically those working in sustainable development.

The EU also engages in the support of social entrepreneurship: The Social Impact Accelerator (SIA) is a €243 million

($270 million) fund that invests in social impact funds that target social enterprises across Europe.[45]

Some countries are making progress in defining new legal forms, along the lines of the benefit corporation in the US, so as to make it easier for impact investors to identify appropriate companies. Italy's recent reform of its social sector includes the introduction of new legal entities similar to benefit corporations in the US and the creation of Impresa Sociale, a model of social enterprise that will allow purpose-driven businesses to be classified as social enterprises, opening up the social sector to private investment. France has introduced similar legislation; its Pacte Law created the new corporate form *société à mission,* allowing a business to include a mission other than profit in its articles of incorporation.[46] Argentina, Brazil and Israel are also in the process of considering similar laws.[47]

We Can Turn the Ocean Liner Around

Citizens care about how their taxes are spent and how their pensions are invested. They care about how their governments address their communities' social and environmental issues – from their schools and hospitals to social care provision and environmental conservation. On a global scale, we are now fully aware of the imminent threat of the global climate crisis, the human and social repercussions of environmental destruction and the disastrous implications of rising inequality for our societies.

Governments are feeling the popular pressure for radical change and know that they need to take urgent action. Ten years ago we did not know what to do to improve our economic system; now, the pieces are in place. As a 2019 OECD report recognizes, governments must play a role in facilitating and nurturing the impact market, by developing standards in measurement and reporting, building market infrastructure and introducing incentives for investors.[48] Even in this politically polarized era, the left and right can agree that we must harness the power of market forces, entrepreneurship and innovation to achieve greater social mobility a fairer distribution of opportunity and social and economic outcomes.

> Ten years ago we did not know what to do to improve our economic system; now, the pieces are in place

We cannot continue to rely on government and philanthropy alone to solve our problems – instead, we need to harness the power of business and investment. Just as US government regulation adapted to the new risk thinking and helped venture capital to grow, funding the Tech Revolution, today government must adapt to the new thinking about risk–return–impact, and use its regulatory power to accelerate its advance. This time, the pay-off for government is greater still, as impact investment effectively puts us on the path to impact economies that are capable of bringing solutions to our great challenges.

Support for impact initiatives across the world has existed on both sides of the political aisle. For example, in the UK the effort around social investment started under the Labour governments of Tony Blair and Gordon Brown, but continued during the Conservative government of David Cameron. In the US, Republican leaders such as Paul Ryan and Todd Young have joined with Democrats like John Delaney to include $100 million in the US budget to fund outcome payments for social impact bonds.[49]

Spending for service provision on the basis of the outcomes achieved appeals to some politicians because it focuses government expenditure on achieving results in cost-effective ways, while others are attracted to the idea of using financial markets to reduce inequality, improve people's lives and preserve the planet. But whatever your ideological motivation, the result is a radically transformed economy that will drive major improvement in lives and the environment. Political leaders who seize this moment will make their names by leading us through a historic transition to a fairer and more effective economic system that is capable of meeting the great challenges of our times.

There is a powerful solution within our grasp

Our world is beset by disquiet and uncertainty, which has frozen many of our governments into inaction. However, there is a powerful solution within our grasp that empowers governments to solve bigger problems, faster: impact.

I believe that in ten or twenty years we will see a significant portion of government spending deployed using pay-for-success approaches to achieve targeted outcomes. Governments will attract private sector capital to fund delivery organizations passionate about tackling our most pressing challenges. Pay-for-outcomes programs will deliver improved results, while those that do not work will naturally come to an end; governments will know what works and what doesn't, and how much they should pay to achieve outcomes that solve social problems.

Most importantly, governments will discover that their best interests are served by using impact investment to lead us to impact economies.

It is time for governments to grasp the new model of risk–return–impact, to progress from piloting impact investment initiatives to driving their advance at scale. The success of the Impact Revolution requires the achievement of three near-term goals: the wide adoption of impact measurement by companies and investors; the creation of a powerful ecosystem to drive investment towards impact-driven companies; and the shift of governments to outcome-based spending.

To quote the nineteenth-century Spanish poet, Antonio Machado, 'There is no path. Paths are made by walking.' It is time for governments to lead us on the new path of impact investment, towards impact economies and impact capitalism.

Chapter 7

THE INVISIBLE HEART OF IMPACT CAPITALISM

There is a will, there is a way, and now is the time to act

All over the world, capitalism and democracy are being forcefully challenged. It is becoming increasingly clear that current levels of inequality are unsustainable and many people around the world, in both developed and emerging countries, are rebelling against the unfair distribution of social, economic and environmental outcomes.

Yet, unaided, governments and philanthropists cannot be expected to bring the urgently needed solutions; and governments are waking up to the fact that they are not always best placed to provide the innovative solutions we need. This explains why impact investment has appeared on the scene – it embodies what is needed if we are to change our economic system for the better. It points the way to an economy that is able to redistribute economic, social and environmental outcomes in a more equitable way. An economy that uses free markets and capital to grow, but also to help those whom rising prosperity has left stranded. Impact investment heralds the Impact Revolution, which promises to be as innovative and disruptive as the Tech Revolution that preceded it.

Inequality today may have some political causes, but it is principally the consequence of our economic system. For more than 200 years, our existing version of capitalism drove prosperity and lifted billions out of poverty, but it no longer fulfills its promise to deliver widespread economic improvement and social progress. Its negative social and environmental consequences have become so great that we can no longer handle them.

In the early stages of our industrial development our governments could cope with the environmental consequences of industrialization, but their scale today is so great that powerful new solutions are required. In my view, we must turn our capitalist system around, so that it delivers systemic social and environmental improvement, move it from what we might call the 'selfish capitalism' of today, which is driven solely by profit, to the 'impact capitalism' of our future, which is driven by profit and impact in equal measure.

To achieve this, we must galvanize the five stakeholder groups we have looked at in different chapters of this book and each play our own individual role in driving real change. What conclusions have we reached during our journey?

1. We cannot solve our social and environmental challenges by merely tinkering with our existing system.

2. We need to bring impact to the center of our economic system, alongside profit, where it can drive the systemic creation of positive outcomes.

3. Impact-weighted accounts for businesses, which dependably reflect their impact, will be the watershed between the risk–return and risk–return–impact paradigms.

4. Investment returns from risk–return–impact will be at least as good as the returns from risk–return, and most likely better.

5. Risk–return–impact thinking is disrupting entrepreneurship, business, investment, philanthropy and government in just as far-reaching a way as technology.

6. The chain-reaction triggered by risk–return–impact thinking is already under way, driven by young consumers, entrepreneurs and employees. They have influenced the behavior of investors, who have joined them in influencing the behavior of businesses, philanthropists and governments.

7. Impact investment beats the path to impact economies through the use of impact measurement; new tools that rely on impact measurement such as SIBs/DIBs and Outcome Funds; new organizations such as impact capital wholesalers; and impact entrepreneurs.

8. Impact capitalism and the impact economies that sustain it will emerge and succeed because they embody the values of a rising generation that understands that our future depends on it.

Powerful new ideas have brought radical change before. In the late eighteenth century, Jean-Jacques Rousseau's *The Social Contract* attacked the idea that monarchs were divinely empowered to rule and argued that the will of the people should give direction to the state. His writings inspired political reforms and revolutions, in France, America and elsewhere. Under the new social contract that was established, democracy came to protect the rights of the individual in the political realm. Our own generation's challenge is to protect the rights of the individual in the social and economic realm.

As Rousseau was launching his political ideas on the world, Adam Smith introduced the theory of the 'invisible hand of markets' in *The Wealth of Nations*. In his view, 'the invisible hand'– a metaphor for individuals acting in their own self-interest within a free market economy – created an equilibrium between the supply and demand for goods, which was in everyone's best interest. His thinking has dominated the economic narrative ever since.

In actual fact, Adam Smith was prouder of the ideas in *The Theory of Moral Sentiments*, published 17 years before *The Wealth of Nations* in 1759. In this earlier work, he sought to provide the moral and ethical foundation for human behavior, postulating that, 'How selfish soever man may be supposed, there are evidently some principles in his nature, which interest him in the fortune of others, and render their happiness necessary to him, though he derives nothing from it, except the pleasure of seeing it.' It is this that constitutes the 'invisible heart of markets'.

As I wrote in this book's introduction, had Smith thought that we could measure what we now call impact, he might have merged the two works and described a single economic system, in which the invisible heart of markets guides their invisible hand.

The new ideas brought by *The Wealth of Nations* helped shift our economic system from mercantilism (which held that countries should use trade and the accumulation of gold to make themselves more powerful), to laissez-faire (the idea that state intervention in economic activity is ill-advised), which prevailed until the 1930s. After the Great Depression, this gave way to John Maynard Keynes's new thinking about a 'managed economy', where the state assumes responsibility for altering public expenditure, interest rates and taxation to maintain full employment.

Then, we had a throwback to laissez-faire with the arrival of Milton Friedman's neoliberalism in the 1980s, and its obsessive focus on governments not interfering with business. Neoliberalist thinking has prevailed from the 1980s through to the 2008 financial crisis, after which we have seen the emergence of new thinking, this time about impact and the need for businesses to recognize their wider obligation to all stakeholders, rather than an exclusive obligation to their shareholders.

This is where the new thinking about risk–return–impact fits in historical terms. The impact economy, where free markets are guided by impact through regulation, legislation and new norms, empowers markets to spread opportunity, reduce inequality and help preserve the planet. A worldwide shift to impact economies, where business and investment decisions are based on risk–return–impact, determines our new global system: impact capitalism.

The watershed between selfish capitalism and impact capitalism will be the arrival of impact-weighted financial accounts that reflect both the impact and financial performance of businesses at the same time; after that watershed, it will be necessary for businesses to demonstrate their impact integrity in order to flourish.

What can each of us do to help bring the Impact Revolution to a tipping point?

What can each of us do – whether as an entrepreneur, investor, business leader, philanthropist, social sector worker or government figure – to help bring the Impact Revolution to a tipping point? Scientists at the Rensselaer Polytechnic Institute in New York have found that if 10 per cent of the population firmly hold something to be true, then eventually the majority of people will adopt this belief.[1]

Here is what each of us can do to get to the 10 per cent tipping point and beyond:

Investors

We saw earlier that changes in regulation can be a huge boost in the financial arena. We must widely replicate the initial breakthrough in the US, where a change in regulation opens the door for trustees of foundations and pension funds to make impact investments.

A change in regulation which would allow pension funds to offer savers the opportunity to participate in ESG and impact investing would be profound and it should be our next objective. One option would be for new regulation across the world to mirror the French '90/10' investment programs, with 90 per cent of the money flowing to ESG and 10 per cent of the money going to impact investments.

The tipping point for investors will be reached, in my view, when 100 prominent pension funds and foundation endowments allocate to impact investment, across all asset classes, 10 per cent of their portfolios. To get there, we will be helped by the rising popular movement among pension contributors to make their pension funds' investments matter.

Philanthropists

As we have seen, impact investment is bringing positive disruption to the 'grants-only' model of foundations and ushering in impact philanthropy. Leaders in the foundation world must lead by setting impact allocations in the portfolios of their endowments that make it possible to invest in impact funds across the world, and by deploying a proportion of their annual grant programs through Outcome Funds.

The tipping point will be reached when 50 of the world's leading foundations establish an allocation of 10 per cent of their endowment to impact investment and an allocation of 10 per cent of their grant programs to Outcome Funds.

The social delivery organizations, which are supported by philanthropists, face challenges regarding their capacity to grow– the vast majority are not set up to deliver services at scale. However, the arrival of impact investment has spurred real change: the leaders of non-profit delivery organizations across the world are now adjusting to the fact that they can raise significant investment capital; but in order to be successful in doing so, they first need to recruit people with the right skills to make themselves investment-ready – and for that they need philanthropic support.

Social delivery organizations should be one of the entrepreneurial engines of this revolution – if their leaders can begin to think in terms of helping the largest number of beneficiaries they possibly can and attracting the necessary impact investment to do so, this will bring a revolution in social sector thinking.

Tipping point here will be reached when 10 per cent of the expenditure of 100 prominent social delivery organizations is funded through outcome-based contracts.

Entrepreneurs

Though millennials are one of the key drivers of the Impact Revolution, in many corners of the world they are still not part of it. We must support the spread of impact entrepreneurship and popularize the notion of the 'impact unicorn', a company that is worth one billion dollars but also improves one billion lives.

Impact entrepreneurship will reach a tipping point when 10 per cent of start-ups integrate measurable impact into their business models and adopt B Corp status.

Big Business

We should not expect the big business sector as a whole to lead the Impact Revolution, just as big companies like IBM did not lead the Tech Revolution. Though IBM dominated the computer market, it didn't recognize the new opportunity that existed until it was about to be overtaken by new competitors. The main reason most big businesses will join this revolution is pressure from their stakeholders: consumers who choose products that create positive impact, and shareholders and employees who pressure them to become impact-driven. Over time, as purpose-driven businesses proliferate, big business will have to follow suit or be overtaken. A tipping point will be reached when 50 of the Fortune Global 500 companies measure their impact performance together with their financial one, and set themselves measurable impact objectives.

Government

The tipping point for governments will be reached when 10 per cent of sub-contracted expenditure and foreign aid is made under outcome-based contracts that attract outside investment and improve the effectiveness of government spending.

As we have learned, each of these stakeholder groups is already on the way to a tipping point. The fact that impact is already a mainstream subject of conversation promises accelerated progress to an overall tipping point in the adoption of risk–return–impact thinking quite soon, perhaps within the next five years. This view is reinforced by the growing understanding that impact investment is the only way to bring the missing $30 trillion needed to achieve the UN's SDGs by 2030.

Impact Investment to Reach the SDGs

As we saw in Chapter 3, there is already a $31 trillion ESG and impact investment pool, equivalent to 15 per cent of global investable assets.

The best way of getting this ESG pool to really contribute to the achievement of the SDGs is to convert it into impact investment. To do this, we must be able to measure and compare the contributions to problems and solutions made by different companies. As we have seen, impact-weighted accounts that link companies' impact to the relevant SDGs are on the way. A clear signal from governments that companies will soon be expected to measure and report their impact through their financial accounts would galvanize companies to look closely at their impact and the data they gather to measure it, and catalyze greater efforts on their part to make positive impact.

As we also saw in Chapter 3, the value of companies quoted on the world's stock exchanges is $75 trillion.[2] If by 2030 one-third of these companies publish impact-weighted financial accounts, which catalyze their efforts to deliver more positive impact, companies valued at $25 trillion would be actively contributing to the achievement of the SDGs.

Bringing impact measurement to the bond market, which as we have previously seen totals $100 trillion, will also have a major effect. The place to start here is with green bonds (climate), which are now being followed by blue (oceans), education, social and gender bonds. For example, Prince Charles, founder of the British Asian Trust, and Richard Hawkes, its CEO, have announced the launch of a $100 million gender bond to provide access to better education, jobs and entrepreneurial opportunities for half a million women and girls in South Asia.[3]

The market for green bonds stands at around $750 billion today; if they and other purpose-driven bonds that measure their impact come to account for 10 per cent of the $100 trillion bond market over the next ten years, this would bring $10 trillion of funding to companies for projects that contribute to the SDGs.

If social and development impact bonds come to account for even 1 per cent of the bond market by 2030, this would represent an additional $1 trillion. And finally, if one-third of the $5 trillion pool comprising venture capital, private equity, real estate and infrastructure came to measure and manage its impact, this would represent another $1.65 trillion. Together, these private asset classes would amount to an additional $2.65 trillion contributing to achievement of the SDGs.

Adding all these numbers up brings us to more than $40 trillion of impact investment, a level that would represent a paradigm shift in the way capitalism operates, effectively harnessing it to tackle social and environmental issues. As impact investment flows grow to this level, they will ingrain risk–return–impact deeply within business and investment thinking, changing behavioral norms, transforming our economic system and bringing us closer to impact economies.

An Idea Whose Time Has Come

It will take at least a decade to transform our system, and the transformation will unfold in stages: starting with impact investment and impact measurement; through the development of impact economies; to a new global system of impact capitalism.

As a first step in this transformation, the world will come to embrace the power of risk–return–impact to help investors and businesses generate solutions to our urgent problems. We will come to understand that when we ignore the damage caused by the private sector, we spend precious resources cleaning up the mess. By contrast, when we harness its power for good, we accelerate social progress and prevent similar messes from occurring in the future.

Then, as a next step, in order to guide the efforts of the private sector to deliver massive positive impact, governments will redefine the purpose of companies to include positive social and environmental impact. In parallel, governments will implement pay-for-outcome approaches in government procurement.

As a third step, governments will introduce policies that require businesses and investors to operate on the basis of risk–return–impact. Reducing inequality inevitably involves the redistribution of income and wealth by government, but this alone will not be sufficient – the redistribution of economic and social outcomes can only come through our economic system. Impact must drive our economies to spread opportunity and positive outcomes more widely, and help those left behind.

The fact is that our existing social contract has expired and we are now in the process of drawing up a new one in the form of impact capitalism. The combined power of financial markets, entrepreneurs and big businesses to bring urgently needed solutions is vastly greater than even the power of governments. We must harness this power. We must reshape capitalism so that it delivers its promise to increase prosperity and social progress for all, spreading meaningful economic opportunity to billions of people, lessening inequality and preserving our planet for future generations.

Impact investing starts the chain reaction needed to reshape our capitalist system, to build a world that values social and environmental impact just as highly as profits. It brings proof that seeking positive impact does not have to mean sacrificing profits – on the contrary, that impact helps deliver higher rates of return; that impact-conscious businesses are more appealing to consumers, talented employees and investors, and more likely to succeed.

Fulfilment comes from a balance between what we do for ourselves and what we do for others. Our motivation for creating positive impact as consumers, employees, entrepreneurs and investors springs from being part of something inspiring that is much bigger than ourselves – helping those in need and preserving our planet.

Envision a world that only moves forward, where inequality is shrinking. Where natural resources are regenerated, and where people can unlock their full potential and benefit from shared prosperity. A world focused not only on minimizing harm, but on doing good. Impact is already bringing change: investors and businesses are becoming socially and environmentally conscious; impact entrepreneurs are gaining access to the impact capital they need to bring life-improving ideas to scale; governments are seeing the value in harnessing the innovation of the private sector; and philanthropists are funding the delivery of tangible outcomes.

It is time for us to raise our voices and make an impact through our choices

It is time for us to raise our voices and make an impact through our choices – from how we work, shop and invest, to how we lobby our governments. Sporadic interventions won't do it; we need systemic change. It is time to accelerate change and demand more.

Impact is an idea whose time has come. Let us move beyond the selfish capitalism of today, overthrow the dictatorship of profit, put impact firmly by its side to keep it in check, and usher in a new era of impact capitalism. Ending the plight of billions and the decline of our planet depend on our urgent action. There is a will. There is a way. And there has never been a greater need or a better time than right now.

GLOSSARY

Accelerator

Start-up accelerators support early-stage, growth-driven companies through education, mentorship, and financing.

Benefit Corporation

The benefit corporation is a US legal form that frees businesses from the obligation to maximize profit, enabling them to seek impact at the same time, without having to fear legal action by shareholders. Without the traditional mandate to maximize financial returns at all cost, benefit corporations are able to make decisions that reflect the interests of their workforce, community and the environment, in addition to being concerned with financial returns.

Blended Finance

Blended finance is the complementary use of grants (or grant-equivalent tools) and other types of financing from private and/or public sources to provide financing to make projects financially viable and/or financially sustainable.

Angel Investor

Angel investors invest in small start-ups or entrepreneurs. The capital angel investors provide may be a one-time investment to help the business propel or an ongoing injection of money to support and carry the company through its difficult early stages.

Development Finance Institution (DFI)

Development Finance Institutions (DFIs) are specialized development banks that are usually majority owned by national governments. DFIs invest in private sector projects in low and middle-income countries to promote job creation and sustainable economic growth.

Development Impact Bond (DIB)

A DIB is a SIB in an emerging country, where foundations and aid organizations step in to pay for outcomes, alongside or instead of the government.

Dormant Accounts

A dormant account is a bank or other account that has become separated from its owner for many years. Dormant accounts are also known as unclaimed assets.

ESG

ESG refers to 'environmental, social and governance' standards that socially conscious investors use to screen investments. Environmental criteria assess how a company performs as a steward of the natural environment. Social criteria assess how a company manages relationships with its employees, suppliers, customers and the communities where it operates. Governance criteria assess a company's leadership, executive pay, audits and internal controls, and shareholder rights. Investors who wish to purchase securities that have been screened for ESG criteria can do so through socially or environmentally responsible investment funds.

Fiduciary Duty

A fiduciary duty is the legal term describing the relationship between two parties that obligates one to act solely in the interest of the other. The party designated as the fiduciary owes the legal duty to a principal, and strict care is taken to ensure no conflict of interest arises between the fiduciary and the principal.

Fintech

Technology that is used in the financial sector to design new ways of delivering financial products and services.

Government Commissioning

Government contracting for social services, that falls under government procurement.

Government Procurement

Procurement is government buying contracts for goods and services from businesses and charitable social delivery organizations.

Green Bond

A green bond is a traditional bond, essentially a loan made by a large number of lenders, including individuals, to a company for the purpose of funding one or more environmental projects. Green bonds are now being followed by blue (oceans), education, social and gender bonds.

High Net Worth Individuals (HNWIs)

High net worth individual (HNWI) is a classification used by the financial services industry to denote an individual or a family with assets above a certain figure.

Impact Capitalism

An economic system, which is driven not just by profit but by impact and profit together, so that it delivers systemic social and environmental improvement. The system encompasses impact economies in which free markets are guided to create positive impact through supportive regulation and legislation, and the widespread measurement of impact. In contrast to the 'selfish capitalism' of today, impact capitalism empowers markets to spread opportunity, reduce inequality and help preserve the planet.

Impact Economy

An impact economy is one where measurement of social and environmental impact is integrated in all economic activity; and central to government, business, investment and consumption decisions.

Impact Investment

Investment that has a strong intention to achieve positive social/environmental outcomes where the outcomes achieved are measured as well as the financial return. Impact investing goes further than ESG investing in two ways: firstly, it aims not just to avoid a negative impact, but also to create a positive one; secondly, it measures the impact it creates.

Impact Investment Ecosystem

The impact investment ecosystem is composed of five building blocks: suppliers of impact capital, intermediaries, demand for impact capital from social sector organizations and purpose-driven businesses, policy and regulation, and impact market builders such as impact wholesalers, social investment banks and consulting and accounting firms. The ecosystem drives the interplay of all impact forces that create positive social and environmental impact.

Impact Investment Wholesalers

An impact investment wholesaler is dedicated to creating measurable impact on people and the planet. It is a large pool of money, sometimes funded by unclaimed assets, that finances impact funds, intermediaries and social enterprises. It drives development of the impact investment market, investing where impact investees are unable to raise money.

Impact Measurement

Measuring social and environmental outcomes in order to maximize them.

Impact-Weighted Accounts

Financial accounts (profit and loss statement and balance sheet) that reflect both the financial performance of a company, and the impact it creates on people and the planet through its products, employment and operations.

Incubator

An incubator is a collaborative program designed to help new start-ups grow their business. Incubators help solve some of the problems commonly associated with running a start-up by potentially providing workspace, seed funding, mentoring, and training.

Institutional Investors

An institutional investor is an organization that invests on behalf of its members, for example a pension fund or insurance company.

Intermediary

An entity (such as a fund) that raises money from impact investors and invests that money in purpose-driven businesses and charitable organizations. An intermediary may also arrange investments and provide advice without actually managing money (such as an impact investment advisor or a broker).

Mission-Related Investment (MRI)

MRIs, in contrast to PRIs, are investments made from the 95 per cent of the endowment, which holds and manages the foundation's assets, rather than from the 5 per cent of it that is given away in grants each year. They are investments that seek social/environmental and financial returns at the same time.

Outcomes-based Contract

An outcomes-based contract is a pay-for-success contract in which providers of public or philanthropic services are rewarded according to the outcomes they achieve. Outcomes-based contracts seek to improve the productivity of delivery by paying only when specific outcomes are achieved.

Outcome Fund

An Outcome Fund is a philanthropic fund that pays for the outcomes achieved by SIBs/DIBs and as a result of other forms of outcomes-based contracts. They can be set up and managed by governments or by independent Outcome Fund managers. Contributors to Outcome Funds can be governments, aid organizations, philanthropic foundations or a combination of all three.

Pay-for-Outcomes

The practice of paying for outcomes achieved by providers that deliver public or philanthropic services. Pay-for-outcomes, also referred to as pay-for-success, is often used to describe securities like social and development impact bonds.

Principles of Responsible Investment (PRIs)

The UN-sponsored Principles for Responsible Investment (PRIs) are a set of six principles that provide a global standard for responsible investing as it relates to environmental, social and corporate governance (ESG) factors. Organizations follow these principles to meet commitments to beneficiaries while aligning investment activities with the broader interests of society.

Program-related Investment (PRI)

An investment made by foundations to support charitable activities that involve the potential return of capital.

Program-related investments include loans, loan guarantees, linked deposits, SIBs/DIBs and even equity investments in charitable organizations or in purpose-driven businesses. Because of their high philanthropic contribution and the high level of financial risk involved, under US regulations, they qualify as grants and count towards the 5 per cent of the endowment's value that must be given away annually.

Public-private Partnerships

Public-private partnerships between a government agency and private-sector company can be used to finance, build and operate projects, such as public transportation networks, parks and convention centers. Social and development impact bonds can be examples of public-private partnerships when a government pays for the outcomes achieved, and private sector investors provide the upfront funding.

Retail Investors

A retail investor, also known as an individual investor, is a non-professional investor who buys and sells securities or funds through traditional or online brokerage firms.

Social Impact Bond (SIB)

A SIB, which is known as a PFS (pay for success) in the United States, an SBB (social benefit bond) in Australia and a social impact contract in France, is not a 'bond' in the traditional sense. It is an outcome-based contract for services between an 'outcome payer' and a delivery organization to achieve social or environmental outcomes. An investor then provides the funding to deliver the services. If results do not meet the targets set in the contract, the investor loses their money, having effectively made a philanthropic donation. If, on the other hand, the targets are met, the investor receives their investment back, with a return that rises with the extent of the outcomes achieved.

Solidarity Fund (France)

Companies with more than 50 employees are obliged to offer their staff, in addition to regular saving schemes, an optional solidarity-savings fund, which allocates 5 to 10% of its assets to eligible (unlisted) social enterprises, and the balance to ESG investments.

Sustainable Development Goals (SDGs)

In 2015, the United Nations launched the Sustainable Development Goals (SDGs) to improve our world by building a more just and sustainable future. By 2030, these goals aim to hit a number of targets across 17 areas, including zero poverty and hunger, water and energy for all, inclusive and equitable quality education, environmental stewardship and protection of human rights.

Unclaimed Assets

Unclaimed assets are money, investments or insurance policies that have become separated from their owners for many years. Unclaimed assets are also referred to as dormant accounts.

Venture Capital

Investment in young high-growth companies, to finance their start-up and growth.

Source

Based on glossary of the GSG report:
Catalysing an Impact Investment Ecosystem: A Policymaker's Toolkit
(January 2019)
https://gsgii.org/reports/catalysing-an-impact-investment-
ecosystem-a-policymakers-toolkit/

———

NOTES

Introduction

1. https://www.ubs.com/global/en/wealth-management/
   uhnw/philanthropy/shaping-philanthropy.html and https://cpl.
   hks.harvard.edu/global-philanthropy-report-perspectives-
   global-financial-sector
2. https://www.academia.edu/32113970/IMPACT_INVESTMENT_
   THE_INVISIBLE_HEART_OF_MARKETS_Harnessing_the_
   power_of_entrepreneurship_innovation_and_capital_for_
   public_good
3. https://ssir.org/articles/entry/should_you_agitate_innovate_
   or_orchestrate

Chapter 1: The Impact Revolution: Risk–Return–Impact

1. http://www.socialvalueuk.org/what-is-social-value/
2. https://www.forbes.com/top-public-companies/list/
3. http://www.bridgesfundmanagement.com/wp-content/
   uploads/2017/12/Bridges-Annual-Impact-Report-2017-v1-web.
   pdf and http://www.bridgesfundmanagement.com/bridges-
   annual-impact-report-2017/
4. Bank accounts that have become separated from their owners
   for a certain length of time, and as a result lie dormant.
5. http://www.telegraph.co.uk/news/uknews/law-and-
   order/8110458/Three-in-four-offenders-stick-to-a-life-of-crime.
   html
6. https://data.ncvo.org.uk/a/almanac15/assets/
7. http://data.foundationcenter.org/
8. https://www.fnlondon.com/articles/why-sir-ronald-cohen-
   deserves-the-nobel-peace-prize-20170801

[9] https://www.brookings.edu/research/impact-bonds-in-developing-countries-early-learnings-from-the-field/ and https://www.gov.uk/guidance/social-impact-bonds#uk-government-outcomes-funds-for-sibs

[10] https://www.wired.com/2015/03/opinion-us-embassy-beijing-tweeted-clear-air/

[11] http://eprints.lse.ac.uk/65393/1/Assessing%20social%20impact%20assessment%20methods%20report%20-%20final.pdf

[12] https://www.gov.uk/guidance/social-impact-bonds

[13] http://www.globalvaluexchange.org/

[14] http://www.globalvaluexchange.org/valuations/8279e41d9e5e0bd8499f2da3

[15] https://www.unpri.org/signatories/signatory-directory

[16] https://www.blackrock.com/hk/en/insights/larry-fink-ceo-letter

Chapter 2: The Age of Impact Entrepreneurship

[1] This opening story was taken from Aryn Baker's 'Zipline's Drones Are Saving Lives', 31 May 2018 – http://time.com/longform/ziplines-drones-are-saving-lives/

[2] https://pando.com/2016/11/10/zipline/

[3] Ibid.

[4] Ibid.

[5] Ibid.

[6] https://www.modernghana.com/news/899872/from-muhanga-to-the-rest-of-rwanda-how-zipline-is-providing.html

[7] https://dronelife.com/2018/04/04/zipline-announces-new-drones/

[8] Ibid.

[9] https://techcrunch.com/2019/05/17/ziplines-new-190-million-funding-means-its-the-newest-billion-dollar-contender-in-the-game-of-drones/

[10] Ibid.

[11] Ibid.

[12] https://www.mirror.co.uk/tech/hi-tech-specs-allow-blind-7756188

13 https://www.orcam.com/en/media/blind-veteran-reads-to-his-sons-using-orcams-technology/

14 https://www.devdiscourse.com/article/international/473713-blind-and-visually-impaired-cast-their-ballots-unassisted-in-israel-election

15 https://www.ft.com/content/3d091920-0970-11e7-ac5a-903b21361b43

16 https://www.ft.com/content/b93ab27a-07e4-11e7-97d1-5e720a26771b

17 https://www.irishtimes.com/business/innovation/myeye-a-glimpse-of-the-future-for-visually-impaired-1.3380963

18 https://pressreleases.responsesource.com/news/96779/visually-impaired-student-is-achieving-independence-with-cutting-edge-artificial-vision/

19 https://www.reuters.com/article/us-tech-orcam-valuation/israeli-visual-aid-company-orcam-valued-at-1-billion-idUSKCN1G326E

20 Ibid.

21 https://www.news.com.au/technology/gadgets/wearables/the-breakthrough-of-the-21st-century-how-this-product-changed-a-blind-womans-life/news-story/74f9881ed0f6f87a8797842bd982d1da

22 https://www.eastersealstech.com/2019/01/04/atu397-carlos-pereira-founder-and-ceo-of-livox/

23 https://solve.mit.edu/challenges/teachers-and-educators/solutions/4677

24 https://www.weforum.org/agenda/2018/01/this-man-made-an-app-so-he-could-give-his-daughter-a-voice/

25 Ibid.

26 https://www.youtube.com/watch?v=MrpL6SrfgA8

27 https://solve.mit.edu/challenges/teachers-and-educators/solutions/4677

28 https://www.schwabfound.org/awardees/carlos-edmar-pereira

29 https://www.forbes.com/companies/tala/?list=fintech/#64ca4ec84c4d

30 https://www.fastcompany.com/40528750/these-entrepreneurs-are-taking-back-your-credit-score-from-the-big-credit-bureaus

31 Ibid.
32 https://techcrunch.com/2018/04/18/with-loans-of-just-10-this-startup-has-built-a-financial-services-powerhouse-in-emerging-markets/
33 https://www.forbes.com/companies/tala/?list=fintech/#64ca4ec84c4d
34 https://www.forbes.com/sites/forbestreptalks/2016/08/29/how-tala-mobile-is-using-phone-data-to-revolutionize-microfinance/#1f8f38f82a9f
35 https://www.fastcompany.com/40528750/these-entrepreneurs-are-taking-back-your-credit-score-from-the-big-credit-bureaus and https://www.forbes.com/sites/forbestreptalks/2016/08/29/how-tala-mobile-is-using-phone-data-to-revolutionize-microfinance/#1f8f38f82a9f
36 https://static1.squarespace.com/static/57687604579fb3ab71469c8f/t/5bdc851b21c67c47f9f9a802/1541178690584/Tala+Impact+Report+-+11.18.pdf
37 https://www.forbes.com/sites/forbestreptalks/2016/08/29/how-tala-mobile-is-using-phone-data-to-revolutionize-microfinance/#1f8f38f82a9f
38 https://www.devex.com/news/a-look-at-digital-credit-in-kenya-and-why-access-alone-is-not-enough-93748
39 https://static1.squarespace.com/static/57687604579fb3ab71469c8f/t/5bdc851b21c67c47f9f9a802/1541178690584/Tala+Impact+Report+-+11.18.pdf
40 https://tala-mobile.squarespace.com/series-c-release
41 https://www.reuters.com/article/us-paypal-tala/paypal-backs-emerging-markets-lender-tala-idUSKCN1MW1MT
42 https://medium.com/tala/with-65m-tala-goes-global-q-a-with-shivani-siroya-founder-ceo-and-female-founders-fund-5c4d0699f350
43 https://academic.oup.com/bioscience/article/67/4/386/3016049
44 https://www.theguardian.com/news/2018/mar/26/the-human-microbiome-why-our-microbes-could-be-key-to-our-health
45 https://www.youtube.com/watch?v=f_P1uoV8R6Q
46 https://www.indigoag.com/product-performance-data

47 https://agfundernews.com/breaking-indigo-raises-250m-series-e-adding-grain-marketplace-to-farm-services-platform.html

48 https://www.youtube.com/watch?v=f_P1uoV8R6Q

49 Ibid.

50 https://www.reuters.com/article/nigeria-unemployment-idUSL5N10T29Q20150902

51 https://www.techcityng.com/tolu-komolafe-andela-superwoman/

52 https://africacheck.org/reports/nigerias-unemployment-rate-18-8-widely-tweeted/

53 https://www.nytimes.com/2017/10/10/business/andela-start-up-coding-africa.html

54 https://www.cnn.com/videos/tv/2016/11/01/exp-gps-1030-andela-interview.cnn

55 https://medium.com/the-andela-way/hello-world-class-completing-the-andela-fellowship-ace88447d27e

56 https://borgenproject.org/tag/tolulope-komolafe/

57 https://venturebeat.com/2019/02/11/andela-will-use-ai-to-pair-african-developers-with-high-growth-startups/

58 https://www.bloomberg.com/news/articles/2019-01-23/al-gore-s-firm-leads-100-million-round-in-african-startup-andela

59 https://www.newyorker.com/magazine/2015/07/20/new-guys

60 https://www.ozy.com/rising-stars/if-she-has-her-way-the-next-bill-gates-will-come-from-lagos/71949

61 https://techcrunch.com/video/andelas-christina-sass-on-growing-tech-talent-in-africa/

62 Ibid.

63 https://www.forbes.com/sites/forbestreptalks/2018/01/12/andela-aims-to-solve-the-developer-shortage-with-tech-workers-from-africa/#45b9af91764e

64 https://techcrunch.com/video/andelas-christina-sass-on-growing-tech-talent-in-africa/

65 https://techmoran.com/2015/06/25/spark-capital-makes-first-african-investmentleads-series-a-funding-for-andela/

66 https://techcrunch.com/video/andelas-christina-sass-on-growing-tech-talent-in-africa/

[67] https://www.prnewswire.com/news-releases/andela-raises-40m-to-connect-africas-engineering-talent-with-global-technology-companies-300533747.html

[68] https://www.economist.com/special-report/2017/11/09/technology-may-help-compensate-for-africas-lack-of-manufacturing

[69] https://www.bloomberg.com/news/articles/2019-01-23/al-gore-s-firm-leads-100-million-round-in-african-startup-andela

[70] https://lifestyle.thecable.ng/tolu-komolafe-andela-programming/

[71] https://www.washingtonpost.com/news/parenting/wp/2017/03/09/reading-writing-and-hunger-more-than-13-million-kids-in-this-country-go-to-school-hungry/

[72] https://www.nytimes.com/2010/01/24/us/24sfpolitics.html?_r=0

[73] https://www.washingtonpost.com/news/parenting/wp/2017/03/09/reading-writing-and-hunger-more-than-13-million-kids-in-this-country-go-to-school-hungry/

[74] https://www.cdc.gov/features/school-lunch-week/index.html

[75] https://www.nytimes.com/2012/09/30/jobs/revolution-foods-chief-on-healthier-school-meals.html

[76] https://www.bostonglobe.com/metro/2017/07/23/fresh-start-for-boston-school-lunches/zt6N1DO2yFC5UwH2x0H1lM/story.html

[77] https://www.fastcompany.com/3039619/revolution-foods

[78] https://www.nytimes.com/2012/09/30/jobs/revolution-foods-chief-on-healthier-school-meals.html

[79] http://time.com/2822774/revolution-foods-steve-case/

[80] https://medium.com/kid-tech-by-collab-sesame/how-revolution-foods-is-democratizing-healthy-living-to-set-kids-up-for-success-b5184973e3e4

[81] http://time.com/2822774/revolution-foods-steve-case/

[82] Ibid.

[83] https://www.fastcompany.com/3039619/revolution-foods

[84] https://www.crunchbase.com/organization/revolution-foods

[85] https://www.bizjournals.com/sanfrancisco/news/2019/01/10/can-healthy-school-lunches-be-a-1-billion-idea.html

[86] https://www.revolutionfoods.com/blog/being-a-b-corp-qa-with-co-founder-kirsten-tobey/

87 https://medium.com/kid-tech-by-collab-sesame/how-revolution-foods-is-democratizing-healthy-living-to-set-kids-up-for-success-b5184973e3e4

88 https://medium.com/kid-tech-by-collab-sesame/how-revolution-foods-is-democratizing-healthy-living-to-set-kids-up-for-success-b5184973e3e4

89 https://bridgesisrael.com/nazid-impact-food/

90 https://www.marketwatch.com/story/this-startup-seeks-to-identify-water-problems-before-they-become-crises-2019-03-22

91 Ibid.

92 https://www.environmentalleader.com/2019/03/179490/

93 https://bombas.com/pages/about-us

94 https://www.elvisandkresse.com/pages/about-us-2

95 https://www.businessinsider.com/london-handbag-fire-hoses-recycled-fashion-accessories-sustainability-2019-5

96 Ibid.

97 Ibid.

98 https://www.bloomberg.com/news/articles/2019–04-17/tesla-s-first-impact-report-puts-hard-number-on-co2-emissions

99 https://thenextweb.com/cars/2018/06/05/this-indian-startup-is-taking-a-shot-at-becoming-the-tesla-of-electric-two-wheelers/

100 https://www.wsj.com/articles/the-fast-and-the-financed-chinas-well-funded-auto-startups-race-to-overtake-tesla-1513498338

101 https://www.bcorporation.net/what-are-b-corps

102 See more examples listed at http://benefitcorp.net/faq

103 https://www.triplepundit.com/2014/03/emerging-legal-forms-allow-social-entrepreneurs-blend-mission-profits/

104 http://benefitcorp.net/policymakers/state-by-state-status

105 https://assets.publishing.service.gov.uk/government/uploads/system/uploads/attachment_data/file/727053/cic-18-6-community-interest-companies-annual-report-2017-2018.pdf and https://www.gov.uk/government/publications/cic-regulator-annual-report-2017-to-2018

106 https://www.ashoka.org/en-IL/about-ashoka

107 http://www.echoinggreen.org/about/

[108] https://endeavor.org/global-board/linda-rottenberg/

Chapter 3: Impact Investing Sets the New Normal

[1] http://www.gsi-alliance.org/wp-content/uploads/2019/03/
GSIR_Review2018.3.28.pdf

[2] https://www.climatebonds.net/2019/10/green-bond
-issuance-tops-200bn-milestone-new-global-record-green-
finance-latest-climate

[3] https://www.climatebonds.net/files/reports/2019_annual_
highlights-final.pdf

[4] https://thegiin.org/assets/Sizing%20the%20Impact%20
Investing%20Market_webfile.pdf

[5] https://www.investopedia.com/advisor-network/articles/
social-returns-just-important-millennial-investors/ and https://
onwallstreet.financial-planning.com/news/millennials-want-
their-investing-to-make-a-difference. Study from 2016

[6] http://www.businessinsider.com/meet-blackrocks-impact-
investing-team-2016–6

[7] https://www.theatlantic.com/business/archive/2017/11/
resource-generation-philanthropy/546350/

[8] https://www.theguardian.com/business/2019/dec/02/
directors-climate-disclosures-tci-hedge-fund

[9] http://people.stern.nyu.edu/adamodar/pdfiles/valrisk/ch4.
pdf (p.8–12)

[10] https://www.ifc.org/wps/wcm/connect/76e6607a-11a4-
4ae8-a36c-7116b3d9dab3/Impactprinciples_booklet_FINAL_
web_4-12-19.pdf?MOD=AJPERES

[11] https://www.impactprinciples.org/signatories-reporting as of
November 2019

[12] https://www.forbes.com/sites/bhaktimirchandani/2019/
04/12/what-you-need-to-know-about-the-ifcs-operating-
principles-for-impact-management/#7da3fd3126b7

[13] https://www.ubs.com/global/en/wealth-management/uhnw/
philanthropy/shaping-philanthropy.html and https://cpl.hks.
harvard.edu/global-philanthropy-report-perspectives-global-
financial-sector

14 https://www.willistowerswatson.com/en-CA/insights/
2019/02/global-pension-assets-study-2019

15 https://bigsocietycapital.fra1.cdn.digitaloceanspaces.com/
media/documents/Pensions_with_Purpose_Final.pdf and
https://bigsocietycapital.com/latest/pensions-purpose/

16 https://www.top1000funds.com/analysis/2017/02/01/
pggm-apg-lead-dutch-sustainability-push/

17 https://www.apg.nl/en/who-is-apg (as of April 2019)

18 https://www.sdgi-nl.org

19 https://news.impactalpha.com/dutch-pension-fund-
moves-from-impact-alignment-to-impact-management-
da2cab1c91c5

20 https://www.top1000funds.com/analysis/2017/02/01/
pggm-apg-lead-dutch-sustainability-push/ and https://www.
top1000funds.com/analysis/2017/08/17/dutch-pension-
funds-embrace-un-goals/

21 https://news.impactalpha.com/dutch-pension-fund-moves-
from-impact-alignment-to-impact-management-da2cab1c91c5

22 https://www.ipe.com/countries/netherlands/engineering-
scheme-introduces-real-assets-portfolio-targeting-25bn
10031069.fullarticle

23 http://impactalpha.com/
global-goals-european-pension-funds/

24 https://www.ipe.com/countries/netherlands/europes-
biggest-pension-fund-to-cut-33bn-of-tobacco-nuclear-
assets/10022647.article and https://www.ipe.com/countries/
netherlands/pgb-to-ditch-tobacco-from-its-investment-
universe/10021218.article

25 https://www.ipe.com/news/esg/uks-nest-adopts-climate-
aware-fund-for-default-strategy/10017699.article

26 https://www.top1000funds.com/2016/12/hsbc-pensions-
innovative-dc-offering/

27 https://www.ipe.com/pensions/investors/how-we-run-our-
money-hsbc-uk-pension-scheme/10020454.article

28 https://pressroom.vanguard.com/nonindexed/HAS18_
062018.pdf

29 https://evpa.eu/uploads/documents/FR-Nugget-90-10-
Funds.pdf

30 https://thephilanthropist.ca/2018/07/more-than-a-million-french-using-their-savings-for-social-good-a-novel-approach-to-impact-investing-in-france/

31 http://www.smf.co.uk/wp-content/uploads/2015/09/Social-Market-FoundationSMF-BSC-030915-Good-Pensions-Introducing-social-pension-funds-to-the-UK-FINAL.pdf

32 https://www.calpers.ca.gov/docs/forms-publications/facts-about.pdf

33 https://www.calpers.ca.gov/page/investments

34 https://www.prnewswire.com/news-releases/assets-of-the-1000-largest-us-retirement-plans-hit-record-level-300402401.html

35 https://www.businessinsider.co.za/climate-action-100-gets-energy-giants-to-commit-to-sustainbility-2019-5

36 https://www.calstrs.com/investments-overview

37 https://www.calstrs.com/sites/main/files/file-attachments/calstrs_21_risk_factors.pdf

38 https://hbr.org/2018/01/why-an-activist-hedge-fund-cares-whether-apples-devices-are-bad-for-kids

39 https://www.ai-cio.com/news/japans-government-pension-fund-returns-4-61--fiscal-q3

40 https://www.youtube.com/watch?v=lz26q6fZ6dk (May 2019)

41 https://www.reuters.com/article/us-japan-gpif-esg/japans-gpif-expects-to-raise-esg-allocations-to-10-percent -ftse-russell-ceo-idUSKBN19Z11Y

42 http://www.ftserussell.com/files/press-releases/worlds-largest-pension-fund-selects-new-ftse-russell-index-integrate-esg

43 https://www.msci.com/documents/10199/60420eeb-5c4e-4293-b378-feab6a2bf77f

44 https://www.verdict.co.uk/private-banker-international/news/exclusive-ubs-tops-2016-global-private-wealth-managers-aum-ranking/

45 https://www.businessinsider.com/ubs-impact-fund-investing-in-bono-2017-7

46 https://citywireamericas.com/news/ubs-wm-americas-appoints-head-of-sustainable-investing/a1005975

47 https://www.ubs.com/global/en/investor-relations/financial-information/annual-reporting/2018.html

48 https://www.ubs.com/global/en/wealth-management/
chief-investment-office/investment-opportunities/
sustainable-investing/2017/breaking-down-barriers-private-
wealth-fund-sdgs.html

49 https://align17.com/

50 https://www.devex.com/news/usaid-announces-a-new-
development-impact-bond-91621

51 https://www.thirdsector.co.uk/british-asian-trust-
announces-worlds-largest-impact-bond-education/finance/
article/1492576

52 https://www.frbsf.org/community-development/files/rikers-
island-first-social-impact-bond-united-states.pdf

53 https://www.goldmansachs.com/media-relations/press-
releases/current/gsam-announcement-7-13-15.html

54 https://www.fa-mag.com/news/goldman-says-esg-investing-
has-gone-mainstream-35138.html?mod=article_inline

55 https://www.bloomberg.com/news/articles/2020-02-26/
carlyle-breaks-from-pack-promising-impact-investing-across-
firm

56 http://www.campdenfb.com/article/growth-millennial-
driven-impact-investing-new-global-family-office-report-2017

57 https://www.morganstanley.com/articles/investing-with-
impact

58 https://www.businesswire.com/news/home/20170613
005829/en/Morgan-Stanley-Launches-Sustainable-Investing-
Education-Financial

59 https://www.ft.com/content/f66b2a9e-d53d-11e8-
a854-33d6f82e62f8

60 https://www.generationim.com/generation-philosophy/#vision

61 https://www.triodos-im.com/

62 https://www.crunchbase.com/organization/
triodos-investment-
management

63 https://www.triodos-im.com/articles/2018/
credo-bank-in-georgia

64 https://www.triodos-im.com/articles/projects/do-it

65 Previously known as 'Bridges Ventures'

66 https://www.bridgesfundmanagement.com/wp-content/
uploads/2019/07/Bridges-Impact-Report-2019-web-print-3.pdf

67 https://www.linkedin.com/company/bridgesfund
management/?originalSubdomain=il
68 https://www.bridgesfundmanagement.com/our-story/
69 http://www.leapfroginvest.com/
70 http://www.dblpartners.vc/about/
71 https://www.crunchbase.com/organization/social-capital
72 http://www.aavishkaar.in/about-us.php#our-company

Chapter 4: Embedding Impact in Business

1 https://www.reuters.com/article/us-danone-outlook-
ceo/danone-looks-to-ride-healthy-food-revolution-wave-
idUSKBN19D1GA
2 https://www.youtube.com/watch?v=PhuEtyH6SK43
3 https://www.just-food.com/interview/danone-ceo-
emmanuelfaber-on-why-industry-mindset-on-health-and-
sustainabilityneeds-to-change-just-food-interview-part-one_
id137124.aspx https://www.youtube.com/watch?v=PhuEty
H6SK4`
4 Ibid.
5 Ibid.
6 https://www.economist.com/business/2018/08/09/danone-
rethinks-the-idea-of-the-firm
7 https://www.businessroundtable.org/business-roundtable-
redefines-the-purpose-of-a-corporation-to-promote-an-
economy-
that-serves-all-americans
8 https://www.businessroundtable.org/about-us
9 https://www.oecd.org/inclusive-growth/businessforinclusive
growth/
10 https://www.oecd.org/newsroom/top-global-firms-commit-
to-tackling-inequality-by-joining-business-for-inclusive-
growth-coalition.htm
11 https://www.unilever.com/sustainable-living/reducing
environmental-impact/greenhouse-gases/innovating-to-
reducegreenhouse-gases/#244-
12 http://www.buycott.com/
13 https://www.globalcitizen.org/en/content/buycott-conscious
consumer-app-of-the-week/

14 http://www.buycott.com/faq
15 http://www.mtv.com/news/2682766/buycott-app-where
    groceries-come-from/
16 https://www.accenture.com/t20181205T121039Z__w__/us-
    en/_acnmedia/Thought-Leadership-Assets/PDF/Accenture-
    CompetitiveAgility-GCPR-POV.pdf#zoom=50
17 https://www.theguardian.com/society/2017/may/17/
    coca-cola-says-sugar-cuts-have-not-harmedsales
18 https://www.confectionerynews.com/Article/2018/05/18/
    Nestle-to-cut-more-sugar-and-salt-in-packaged-foods
19 https://www.just-food.com/news/mars-launches-healthy
    snacks-goodnessknows_id130089.aspx
20 https://www.foodbev.com/news/mars-buys-minority
    stake-kind-response-healthier-snacking/
21 Available as of 2018 in: UK, Ireland, Germany, France, the
    Netherlands, Switzerland, Brazil, Argentina and Uruguay.
22 Ibid.
23 https://www.nestle.com/csv/impact/environment
24 https://www.environmentalleader.com/2009/05/new-
    dasani-bottle-made-partially-of-plant-material/
25 https://www.environmentalleader.com/2015/06/coca-
    colaproduces-worlds-first-100-plant-basedpet-bottle/
26 https://globenewswire.com/news-release/2016/05/31/
    844530/0/en/Bio-Based-Polyethylene-Terephthalate-PET-
    Market-size-over-13-Billion-by-2023-Global-Market-Insights-
    Inc.html
27 https://www.accenture.com/t20181205T121039Z__w__/
    us-en/_acnmedia/Thought-Leadership-Assets/PDF/
    Accenture-CompetitiveAgility-GCPR-POV.pdf#zoom=50
28 https://www.forbes.com/sites/andersonantunes/2014/
    12/16/brazils-natura-the-largest-cosmetics-maker-in-latin-
    america-becomes-a-b-corp/#7d0114c125a2
29 http://www.conecomm.com/research-blog/2016-millennial-
    employee-engagement-study
30 Ibid. and http://millennialemployeeengagement.com/
    Methodology:
    The 2016 Cone Communications Millennial Employee
    Engagement Study presents the findings of an online survey
    conducted April 11–20, 2016 by Toluna among a random

sample of 1,020 adults, employed at companies with 1,000 employees or more, comprising 510 men and 510 women, ages 20+. The margin of error associated with a sample of this size is ± 3 per cent at a 95 per cent level of confidence.

[31] https://hbr.org/2011/01/the-big-idea-creating-shared-value
[32] https://www.sharedvalue.org/about-shared-value
[33] https://www.huffpost.com/entry/the-big-idea-creating-sha_b_815696
[34] https://money.cnn.com/magazines/fortune/fortune_archive/2007/02/19/8400261/index.htm
[35] Ibid.
[36] Laura Michelini, 'Social Innovation and New Business Models: Creating Shared Value in Low-Income Markets', *Print*, 2012, p.71
[37] https://www.bloomberg.com/news/articles/2008–04-28/danone-innovates-to-help-feed-the-poorbusinessweek-business-news-stock-market-and-financial-advice
[38] http://content.time.com/time/magazine/article/0,9171,2010077,00.html
[39] Ibid.
[40] Carol Matlack, 'Danone Innovates to Help Feed the Poor', *BusinessWeek Online*, 23 April 2008,http://search.ebscohost.com.ezp-prod1.hul.harvard.edu/login.aspx?direct=true&db=heh&AN=31863578&site=ehost-live&scope=site
[41] http://content.time.com/time/magazine/article/0,9171,2010077,00.html
[42] http://www.danonecommunities.com/index.php/portfolio_page/grameen-damone-food-limited/
[43] https://www.ncbi.nlm.nih.gov/pmc/articles/PMC3671231/ – according to a study by the Johns Hopkins Bloomberg School of Public Health, conducted between 2008 and 2011
[44] http://content.time.com/time/magazine/article/0,9171,2010077,00.html
[45] http://www.danonecommunities.com/
[46] http://www.danonecommunities.com/index.php/alleviate-poverty-fr/
[47] http://www.livelihoods.eu/es/about-us/
[48] Ibid.
[49] Ibid.
[50] https://vimeo.com/36737411

[51] Ibid.

[52] Ibid.

[53] https://www.fastcompany.com/40557647/this-food-giant-is-now-the-largest-b-corp-in-the-world

[54] http://www.wealthandgiving.org/perspectives/2019/2/27/seeking-impact-five-years-on

[55] http://www.danone.com/en/for-all/our-mission-in-action/our-unique-company/alimentation-revolution/

[56] https://www.fooddive.com/news/danone-completes-acquisition-of-organic-foods-producer-whitewave/440356/

[57] https://www.reuters.com/article/us-danone-outlook-ceo/danone-looks-to-ride-healthy-food-revolution-wave-idUSKBN19D1GA

[58] Ibid.

[59] https://www.mckinsey.com/~/media/McKinsey/Business%20Functions/Sustainability/Our%20Insights/Toward%20a%20circular%20economy%20in%20food/Toward%20a%20circular%20economy%20in%20food.ashx

[60] http://iar2017.danone.com/vision-and-ambition/contribution-to-the-uns-sdgs/

[61] https://www.danone.com/impact/planet/towards-carbon-neutrality.html

[62] https://www.mckinsey.com/~/media/McKinsey/Business%20Functions/Sustainability/Our%20Insights/Toward%20a%20circular%20economy%20in%20food/Toward%20a%20circular%20economy%20in%20food.ashx

[63] https://www.wsj.com/articles/danones-deputy-ceo-faber-to-become-chief-executive-1409677620

[64] https://www.youtube.com/watch?v=PhuEtyH6SK4

[65] https://www.fastcompany.com/3068681/how-chobani-founder-hamdi-ulukaya-is-winning-americas-culture-war

[66] Ibid.

[67] Ibid.

[68] Ibid.

[69] Ibid.

[70] https://www.ted.com/talks/hamdi_ulukaya_the_anti_ceo_playbook/transcript?language=en

[71] Ibid.

72 https://money.cnn.com/2016/01/20/news/refugees-business-davos-opinion/index.html
73 https://www.fastcompany.com/3068681/how-chobani-founder-hamdi-ulukaya-is-winning-americas-culture-war
74 https://www.nytimes.com/2018/08/24/business/hamdi-ulukaya-chobani-corner-office.html
75 https://www.nytimes.com/2011/02/17/business/media/17adco.html
76 https://www.nytimes.com/2018/08/24/business/hamdi-ulukaya-chobani-corner-office.html
77 Ibid.
78 https://assets.ctfassets.net/3s6ohrza3ily/5Bry9Rm Mqnd4dF0Yxr8Vy/bbc8cc7867a831c569b355169325354e/COMP_2019_Sustainability_Project_v17.pdf
79 Ibid.
80 Ibid.
81 https://www.evesun.com/progress_folder/2019/pdf/progress9.pdf
82 Ibid.
83 https://www.nytimes.com/2016/04/27/business/a-windfall-for-chobani-employees-stakes-in-the-company.html
84 https://www.forbes.com/sites/simonmainwaring/2018/08/27/how-chobani-builds-a-purposeful-culture-around-social-impact/#19e09b6e20f7
85 https://www.inc.com/christine-lagorio/chobani-founder-hamdi-ulukaya-founders-project.html
86 https://www.nationalgeographic.com/news/2017/07/plastic-produced-recycling-waste-ocean-trash-debris-environment/
87 Ibid.
88 http://www3.weforum.org/docs/WEF_The_New_Plastics_Economy.pdf
89 https://www.adidas-group.com/media/filer_public/8e/f1/8ef142c7-ac01-4cb3-b375-875106168555/2019_adidas_x_parley_qa_en.pdf
90 https://www.cnbc.com/2018/03/14/adidas-sold-1-million-shoes-made-out-of-ocean-plastic-in-2017.html
91 https://www.racked.com/2018/3/15/17124138/adidas-recycled-plastic-parley

92 https://qz.com/quartzy/1598089/adidass-futurecraft-loop-is-a-zero-waste-sustainable-sneaker

93 https://www.engadget.com/2019/04/17/adidas-futurecraft-loop-recycled-running-shoes-sustainability-speedfactory/

94 https://www.fastcompany.com/90335038/exclusive-adidass-radical-new-shoe-could-change-how-the-world-buys-sneakers

95 Ibid.

96 Ibid.

97 Ibid.

98 Ibid.

99 https://www.engadget.com/2019/04/17/adidas-futurecraft-loop-recycled-running-shoes-sustainability-speedfactory/

100 http://highlights.ikea.com/2018/facts-and-figures/home/index.html

101 https://www.ikea.com/us/en/about_ikea/newsitem/022615_pr_making-solid-wood

102 https://www.reuters.com/article/us-ikea-sustainability/ikea-to-use-only-renewable-and-recycled-materials-by-2030-idUSKCN1J31CD

103 https://www.youtube.com/watch?v=rRXNRq5P9O0

104 https://www.ikea.com/ms/en_US/pdf/people_planet_positive/IKEA_Sustainability_Strategy_People_Planet_Positive_v3.pdf

105 https://news.theceomagazine.com/news/ikea-new-bench mark-renewable-furniture/

106 https://www.ikea.com/ms/en_US/pdf/people_planet_positive/IKEA_Sustainability_Strategy_People_Planet_Positive_v3.pdf

107 https://ftalphaville.ft.com/2019/02/20/1550638802000/Dis-assembling-IKEA-/

108 https://www.epa.gov/facts-and-figures-about-materials-waste-and-recycling/durable-goods-product-specific-data#FurnitureandFurnishings

109 https://www.bluebulbprojects.com/measureofthings/results.php?amt=9690000&comp=weight&unit=tns&searchTerm=9690000+tons

[110] https://news.globallandscapesforum.org/32098/ikea-assembles-plan-to-reduce-emissions-in-the-atmosphere-by-2030/

[111] Ibid.

[112] https://www.ft.com/content/da461f24-261c-11e9-8ce6-5db4543da632

[113] Ibid.

[114] https://www.ft.com/content/da461f24-261c-11e9-8ce6-5db4543da632

[115] Ibid.

[116] https://www.dwell.com/article/ikea-gunrid-air-purifying-curtains-81cf8714

[117] https://www.ikea.com/ms/en_AU/this-is-ikea/people-and-planet/sustainable-life-at-home/index.html

[118] http://highlights.ikea.com/2017/circular-economy/index.html

[119] https://www.fastcompany.com/90236539/ikea-is-quickly-shifting-to-a-zero-emissions-delivery-fleet

[120] https://www.consciouscapitalism.org/heroes/b-lab-founders

[121] http://b-analytics.net/content/company-ratings

[122] George Serafeim, DG Park, David Freiberg, T. Robert Zochowski "Corporate Environmental Impact: Measurement, Data and Insights" Harvard Business School Working Paper, Forthcoming March 2020. All emissions data come from Bloomberg and/or Thomson Reuters, and for the emissions data that are missing in one (or either) of the two databases, data from Exiobase is used to impute the values. Those emissions data (in volumes) are then multiplied with EPS monetary estimates (Steen, "Monetary Valuation of Environmental Impacts" CRC Press, 2019), which are also publicly available data

[123] *For calculations of environmental costs:* George Serafeim, DG Park, David Freiberg, T. Robert Zochowski "Corporate Environmental Impact: Measurement, Data and Insights" Harvard Business School Working Paper, Forthcoming March 2020. *For Pepsi-Co Water Usage:* Bloomberg and Thomson Reuters Databases. *Water prices:* Waterfund, LLC. *For Coca-Cola Water Usage:* P.62 of Coca-Cola's 2018 Sustainability Report. Web: https://www.coca-colacompany.com/content/dam/journey/us/en/policies/pdf/safety-health/coca-cola-business-and-sustainability-report-2018.pdf

124 *For environmental cost calculations:* George Serafeim, DG Park, David Freiberg, T. Robert Zochowski "Corporate Environmental Impact: Measurement, Data and Insights" Harvard Business School Working Paper, Forthcoming March 2020. *For Exxon GHG emissions and water usage values:* Bloomberg Database. *For Royal Dutch Shell and BP GHG emissions and water usage values:* Bloomberg and Thomson Reuters databases

125 *For calculations of environmental costs:* George Serafeim, DG Park, David Freiberg, T. Robert Zochowski "Corporate Environmental Impact: Measurement, Data and Insights" Harvard Business School Working Paper, Forthcoming March 2020. *For Daimler's GHG emissions:* Thomson Reuters. *For General Motors GHG emissions:* Both Bloomberg and Thomson Reuters. *For Ford GHG emissions:* Both Bloomberg and Thomson Reuters. *For Daimler, General Motors and Ford disclosed sales:* Worldscope

126 *For calculations of environmental costs:* George Serafeim, DG Park, David Freiberg, T. Robert Zochowski "Corporate Environmental Impact: Measurement, Data and Insights" Harvard Business School Working Paper, Forthcoming March 2020. *For Ford fuel economy of passenger fleet, tail pipe emissions, sales volume:* "SASB Index 2018/19". Ford. Web. https://corporate.ford.com/microsites/sustainability-report-2018-19/assets/files/sr18-sasb.pdf. *For annual mileage:* Based on industry assumptions from the US Department of Transportation's Federal Highway Administration. https://www.fhwa.dot.gov/ohim/onh00/bar8.htm

127 "General Mills marks 10 years of health improvements". General Mills News Releases. 2015 Feb 19. Web. https://www.generalmills.com/en/News/NewsReleases/Library/2015/February/health-metric

128 General Mills Form 10-K for 2018

129 US Dietary Guidelines

130 Dariush Mozaffarian et al. "Trans Fatty Acids and Cardiovascular Disease". The New England Journal of Medicine. 2006 April 13. Web. https://www-nejm-org.ezp-prod1.hul.harvard.edu/doi/full/10.1056/NEJMra054035?url_ver=Z39.88-2003&rfr_id=ori%3Arid%3Acrossref.org&rfr_dat=cr_pub%3Dpubmed

131 https://www.ft.com/content/3f1d44d9-094f-4700-989f-616e27c89599

132 https://www.goodreads.com/quotes/43237-it-s-only-whenthe-tide-goes-out-that-you-learn

Chapter 5: The Dawn of Impact Philanthropy

1   https://www.bridgespan.org/bridgespan/images/articles/how-nonprofits-get-really-big/How-Nonprofits-Get-Really-Big.pdf?ext=.pdf

2   http://www.nonprofitfinancefund.org/sites/default/files/nff/docs/2015-survey-brochure.pdf

3   http://www.urban.org/sites/default/files/publication/43036/411404-Building-a-Common-Outcome-Framework-To-Measure-Nonprofit-Performance.PDF

4   https://www.gov.uk/government/uploads/system/uploads/attachment_data/file/486512/social-impact-bond-pilot-peterborough-report.pdf

5   https://metro.co.uk/2017/08/10/what-happens-when-you-finally-get-released-from-jail-one-former-prisoner-explains-6831114/ and https://www.nacro.org.uk/resettlement-advice-service/support-for-individuals/advice-prisoners-people-licence-sex-offenders-mappa/advice-for-prisoners/

6   Ultimately the Peterborough bond will pay out 7.5 percent. After five years and two cohorts of 1,000 prisoners each, the British government decided to refashion the Probation Office so as to reduce reoffending and the cost to the prison service, and changed the SIB model to a fee-for-service model.

7   https://www.brookings.edu/wp-content/uploads/2019/01/Global-Impact-Bonds-Snapshot-March-2020.pdf

8   Ibid.

9   Ibid.

10 https://www.bridgesfundmanagement.com/uks-first-social-impact-bond-fund-achieves-final-close-25m/ and https://www.bridgesfundmanagement.com/bridges-closes-second-social-outcomes-fund-at-extended-hard-cap-of-35m/

11 https://www.bridgesfundmanagement.com/outcomes-contracts/

12 https://www.bridgesfundmanagement.com/outcomes-contracts/

13 A Newcastle University evaluation in the *British Medical Journal* showed improved well-being, and a publication from Newcastle and Gateshead Clinical Commissioning Group showed a reduction in costs.

14 https://golab.bsg.ox.ac.uk/knowledge-bank/project-data base/fair-chance-fund-west-yorkshire-fusion-housing/

15 https://www.youtube.com/watch?v=sJ-OfYW0hs&feature= youtu.be

16 https://www.kirkleesbetteroutcomespartnership.org/

17 https://impactalpha.com/prudential-kresge-and-steve-ballmer-back-maycomb-capitals-pay-for-success-fund/

18 https://www.livingcities.org/blog/1203-how-massachusetts-s-new-pfs-project-will-help-make-the-american-dream-a-reality

19 https://www.nytimes.com/2007/02/27/education/27esl.html and https://socialfinance.org/wp-content/uploads/MAPath ways_FactSheet.pdf

20 https://thewell.worlded.org/the-massachusetts-pathways-to-economic-advancement-pay-for-success-project/

21 Social Finance US.

22 https://thewell.worlded.org/the-massachusetts-pathways-to-economic-advancement-pay-for-success-project/

23 Ibid.

24 Brookings Institution Global Impact Bond Database,16 January 2020.

25 http://govinnovator.com/emily_gustaffson_wright/

26 https://www.un.org/press/en/2019/dsgsm1340.doc.htm

27 http://instiglio.org/educategirlsdib/wp-content/uploads/ 2015/09/Educate-Girls-DIB-Sept-2015.pdf

28 http://www.instiglio.org/en/girls-education-india/

29 https://www.brookings.edu/blog/education-plus-development/2018/07/13/worlds-first-development-impact-bond-for-education-shows-successful-achievement-of-outcomes-in-its-final-year/

30 http://instiglio.org/educategirlsdib/wp-content/uploads/ 2018/07/Educate-Girls-DIB_results_brochure_final-2.pdf

31 Ibid.

[32] https://www.brookings.edu/wp-content/uploads/2019/01/Global-Impact-Bonds-Snapshot-March-2020.pdf

[33] https://www.brookings.edu/research/impact-bonds-in-developing-countries-early-learnings-from-the-field/

[34] https://www.devex.com/news/icrc-launches-world-s-first-humanitarian-impact-bond-90981

[35] *Learning Generation: Investing in education for a changing world*, The Education Commission, 2017.

[36] https://www.livemint.com/Education/XRdJDgsAbwnSAH8USzyCWM/11-million-development-impact-bonds-launched-to-improve-edu.html, https://www.brookings.edu/blog/education-plus-development/2018/09/25/a-landmark-month-for-impact-bonds-in-education/, https://indiaincgroup.com/prince-charles-backs-new-education-bond-india/ and https://www.britishasiantrust.org/our-impact/innovative-finance

[37] https://www.socialfinance.org.uk/projects/liberia

[38] Ibid.

[39] In their book, *Getting Beyond Better: How Social Entrepreneurship Works*.

[40] https://www.fordfoundation.org/ideas/equals-change-blog/posts/unleashing-the-power-of-endowments-the-next-great-challenge-for-philanthropy/

[41] https://www.rockefellerfoundation.org/our-work/initiatives/innovative-finance/

[42] https://obamawhitehouse.archives.gov/blog/2016/04/21/steps-catalyze-private-foundation-impact-investing

[43] http://www.legislation.gov.uk/ukpga/2016/4/section/15/enacted

[44] https://www.appositecapital.com/mission/

[45] https://www.gsttcharity.org.uk/who-we-are/our-finances/how-we-are-financed/our-endowment and https://www.gsttcharity.org.uk/what-we-do/our-strategy/other-assets/property-and-estates

[46] Mission-Related Investment refers to the use of investments by foundations as tools to achieve their philanthropic goals.

[47] http://www.fordfoundation.org/ideas/equals-change-blog/posts/unleashing-the-power-of-endowments-the-next-great-challenge-for-philanthropy/

NOTES

48 https://nonprofitquarterly.org/can-ford-foundations-1-billion-impact-investing-commitment-alter-field/
49 https://www.fordfoundation.org/ideas/equals-change-blog/posts/unleashing-the-power-of-endowments-the-next-great-challenge-for-philanthropy/
50 https://efc.umd.edu/assets/m2e/pri_final_report_8-05-13.pdf
51 https://www.fastcompany.com/40525515/how-the-ford-foundation-is-investing-in-change
52 Ibid.
53 https://ssir.org/articles/entry/eight_myths_of_us_philanthropy and http://data.foundationcenter.org/#/foundations/all/nationwide/top:assets/list/2015
54 https://www.fastcompany.com/40525515/how-the-ford-foundation-is-investing-in-change
55 https://www.packard.org/wp-content/uploads/2015/10/Packard_MIR_2015OCT51.pdf
56 https://mcconnellfoundation.ca/impact-investing/
57 https://mustardseedmaze.vc/
58 https://knowledge.wharton.upenn.edu/article/from-backstreet-to-wall-st-ep-09/
59 http://www.blueorchard.com/sasakawa-peace-foundation-invest-blueorchards-flagship-fund/
60 https://www.forbes.com/sites/annefield/2015/02/26/f-b-heron-foundation-is-going-all-in/#6d2f79386d2f
61 https://www.forbes.com/sites/annefield/2017/03/30/mission-accomplished-how-the-heron-foundation-went-all-in/#405717a04d17
62 Ibid.
63 https://nonprofitquarterly.org/nathan-cummings-no-longer-just-experimenting-impact-investing/
64 https://www.top1000funds.com/2019/05/foundations-should-invest-for-impact/
65 https://www.forbes.com/sites/laurengensler/2015/11/06/lisa-charly-kleissner-kl-felicitas-impact-investing/#3fa5c38138e7
66 https://toniic.com/t100-powered-ascent-report/
67 Ibid.
68 http://www.toniic.com/100-impact-network/

[69] https://www.bridgespan.org/insights/library/remarkable-givers/profiles/pierre-omidyar/don%e2%80%99t-start-a-foundation-pierre-omidyar-ignores-e

[70] Ibid.

[71] Ibid.

[72] https://www.omidyar.com/financials – The total amount committed since inception is $1.53 billion+. For-profit investments since inception: $713 million. Non-profit grants since inception: $822 million.

[73] https://www.bridgespan.org/insights/blog/give-smart/impact-investing-ebay-founder-pierre-omidyar

[74] http://skoll.org/about/about-skoll/

[75] Ibid.

[76] https://thegiin.org/research/spotlight/investor-spotlight-capricorn-investment-group

[77] https://www.saildrone.com/

[78] https://www.gatesfoundation.org/How-We-Work

[79] https://sif.gatesfoundation.org/what-we-do/ Note that investments from the fund are structured as 'program-related investments', which is a defined term in the US Internal Revenue Code that governs charitable investments made by a private foundation.

[80] http://www.investwithimpact.co/principal-venture-capital-bill-melinda-gates-foundation/

[81] https://sif.gatesfoundation.org/impact-stories/empowering-women-strengthening-families/

[82] https://beyondtradeoffs.economist.com/improving-lives-innovative-investments

[83] http://www.investwithimpact.co/principal-venture-capital-bill-melinda-gates-foundation/

[84] Note: Wealth valued at $45 billion at time of founding https://www.businessinsider.com/mark-zuckerberg-giving-away-99-of-his-facebook-shares-2015-12

[85] https://www.facebook.com/notes/mark-zuckerberg/a-letter-to-our-daughter/10153375081581634/

[86] https://www.macfound.org/press/press-releases/150-million-catalytic-capital-help-address-critical-social-challenges/

87 https://www.forbes.com/sites/kerryadolan/2019/04/16/
    questioning-big-philanthropy-at-the-skoll-world-forum-is-it-
    too-powerful-and-out-of-touch/#375764b76253
88 https://www.bertelsmannstiftung.de/fileadmin/files/user_
    upload/Market_Report_SII_in_Germany_2016.pdf
89 https://www.social finance-org-uk/resources/publications/
    portuguese-social-investment-taskforce-blueprint-portugal
    %22%80%99s-emerging-social

Chapter 6: Government: Solving Bigger Problems, Faster

1   https://digitalcommons.pepperdine.edu/cgi/viewcontent.
    cgi?article=2448&context=plr
2   https://www.thebhc.org/sites/default/files/beh/BEHprint/
    v023n2/p0001-p0026.pdf
3   'Catalysing an Impact Investment Ecosystem'
4   https://www.equalityhumanrights.com/en/advice-and-
    guidance/reporting-requirements-uk, https://
    www.theguardian.com/sustainable-business/
    eu-reform-listed-companies-report-
    environmental-social-impact and
    https://carboncredentials.com/
    the-uk-transposition-of-the-non-financial-reporting-directive/
5   https://www.globalelr.com/2019/04/eu-issues-new-
    sustainable-investment-disclosure-rules/
6   Ibid.
7   https://www.gov.uk/government/publications/social-impact-
    bonds-unit-cost-data
8   http://gsgii.org/wp-content/uploads/2018/10/GSG-Paper-
    2018-Policy.pdf
9   https://onevalue.gov.pt/?parent_id=25
10 http://www.globalvalueexchange.org/news/b07bcb501c
11 https://group.bnpparibas/en/news/social-impact-contracts-
    bnp-paribas-invests-social-innovation
12 http://gsgii.org/wp-content/uploads/2018/10/GSG-Paper-
    2018-Policy.pdf
13 Ibid.

14 https://www.socialventures.com.au/sva-quarterly/how-government-can-grow-social-impact-investing/
15 https://commonslibrary.parliament.uk/research-briefings/cbp-7585/
16 'Bridges Fund Management – Social Outcomes Contracts: An Overview', 2019
17 https://www.csis.org/analysis/leveraging-impact-investment-global-development
18 https://www.gouvernement.fr/sites/default/files/locale/piece-jointe/2019/07/g7_financing_for_sustainable_development_declaration_cle0973b7.pdf
19 http://www.theimpactprogramme.org.uk/
20 https://www.cdcgroup.com/en/catalyst/
21 http://villageenterprise.org/our-impact/development-impact-bond/
22 https://www.devex.com/news/new-dib-brings-in-big-donors-provides-biggest-test-of-model-to-date-91137
23 https://www.bridgesfundmanagement.com/village-enterprise-closes-investment-for-first-development-impact-bond-for-poverty-alleviation-in-sub-saharan-africa/
24 https://www.civilsociety.co.uk/news/government-takes-next-steps-in-releasing-billions-of-pounds-in-dormant-assets.html
25 https://bigsocietycapital.com/impact-stories/
26 http://gsgii.org/wp-content/uploads/2018/10/GSG-Paper-2018-Wholesalers.pdf
27 https://www.reuters.com/article/us-japan-economy-impact-investment/japan-urged-to-tap-dormant-bank-accounts-to-promote-impact-investment-idUSKCN1G316H
28 http://gsgii.org/wp-content/uploads/2018/10/GSG-Paper-2018-Policy.pdf
29 https://www.gov.ie/en/publication/f24ad0-dormant-accounts-action-plan-2019/
30 https://impactinvesting.marsdd.com/unclaimed-assets/
31 https://nextcity.org/daily/entry/sba-program-seeks-to-change-venture-capital and https://independentsector.org/news-post/the-federal-government-and-impact-investing/
32 https://www.willistowerswatson.com/en-CA/insights/2019/02/global-pension-assets-study-2019

33 https://www.bigsocietycapital.com/what-we-do/current-projects/social-investment-tax-relief/get-sitr#SITR-case-studies

34 Depending on the type/length of investment: https://www.tax policycenter.org/briefing-book/what-are-opportunity-zones-and-how-do-they-work

35 As long as you do not sell your shares for five years. https://finansol.org/en/how-to-become-a-solidarity-based-saver-or-investor.php

36 http://gsgii.org/wp-content/uploads/2018/10/GSG-Paper-2018-Policy.pdf

37 https://www.finansol.org/_dwl/social-finance.pdf

38 Approximation (https://www.poundsterlinglive.com/bank-of-england-spot/historical-spot-exchange-rates/gbp/GBP-to-USD-1981)

39 Approximation (https://fxtop.com/en/historical-currency-converter.php?)

40 https://access-socialinvestment.org.uk/us/the-story-so-far/ and https://www.socialventures.com.au/sva-quarterly/how-government-can-grow-social-impact-investing/

41 http://koreabizwire.com/govt-to-boost-policy-support-for-social-impact-investments/116052

42 http://gsgii.org/wp-content/uploads/2018/10/GSG-Paper-2018-Policy.pdf

43 https://docs.jobs.gov.au/system/files/doc/other/sedife valuation.pdf

44 http://impactstrategist.com/case-studies/social-enterprise-development-investment-funds/

45 http://gsgii.org/wp-content/uploads/2018/10/GSG-Paper-2018-Policy.pdf

46 https://ssir.org/articles/entry/french_law_revisits_corporate_purpose

47 http://gsgii.org/wp-content/uploads/2018/10/GSG-Paper-2018-Policy.pdf

48 https://www.devex.com/news/opinion-the-impact-imperative-for-sustainable-development-finance-94142

49 https://www.responsible-investor.com/home/article/pay_for_success_the_latest_thinking_on_social_impact_bonds/

Chapter 7: The Invisible Heart of Impact Capitalism

[1] https://news.rpi.edu/luwakkey/2902

[2] According to the Securities Industry and Financial Markets Association (SIFMA).

[3] https://www.bloomberg.com/news/articles/2019-02-05/british-prince-meets-bond-markets-for-women-empowerment-in-asia

INDEX

ABOUT THE AUTHOR

Sir Ronald Cohen is a pioneering philanthropist, venture capitalist, private equity investor and social innovator, who is driving forward the global Impact Revolution.

He serves as Chairman of the Global Steering Group for Impact Investment and The Portland Trust. He is a co-founder of Social Finance UK, USA and Israel; and co-founder Chair of Bridges Fund Management and Big Society Capital. He chaired the G8 Social Impact Investment Taskforce (2013–15), the UK Social Investment Task Force (2000–10) and the UK's Commission on Unclaimed Assets (2005-2007). In 2012 he received the Rockefeller Foundation's Innovation Award for Social Finance.

He was the co-founder and Executive Chairman of Apax Partners Worldwide LLP (1972-2005), a global private equity firm, and co-founder and Chairman of the British Venture Capital Association. He is former director of the Harvard Management Company, and a former member of the Harvard University Board of Overseers and of the University of Oxford Investment Committee.

Oxford and Harvard educated, Sir Ronald was born in Egypt and left as a refugee at the age of 11, when his family came to the UK. He is based in Tel Aviv, London and New York.